Simply Stylish

Crystal Jewelry

From the publisher of *Bead Style* magazine

KALMBACH BOOKS

20

Kalmbach Books
21027 Crossroads Circle
Waukesha, Wisconsin 53186
www.Kalmbach.com/Books

Published in 2012
16 15 14 13 12   1 2 3 4 5

Manufactured in the United States of America

ISBN: 978-0-87116-445-2

The material in this book has appeared previously in *Bead
Style* magazine. *Bead Style* is registered as a trademark.

Editor: *Elisa Neckar*
Technical Editor: *Karin Van Voorhees*
Proofreader: *Erica Swanson*
Art Director: *Lisa Bergman*
Layout Designers: *Rebecca Markstein and Tom Ford*
Photographers: *Bill Zuback and Jim Forbes*

Library of Congress Cataloging-in-Publication Data

Simply stylish crystal jewelry / from the publisher of Bead Style
magazine.

    p. : col. ill. ; cm. – (Simply stylish)

"The material in this book has appeared previously in Bead
Style magazine."–T.p. verso.

ISBN: 978-0-87116-445-2

1. Beadwork–Handbooks, manuals, etc. 2. Jewelry making–
Handbooks, manuals, etc. 3. Crystals. I. Kalmbach Publishing
Company. II. Title: Crystal jewelry III. Title: Bead Style
Magazine.

TT860 .S56 2012
745.594/2

CONTENTS

BASICS

PROJECTS

56

62

Introduction

Sparkle.

Sparkle, sparkle, sparkle. If there's one word that's used over and over again to describe the allure of crystals, it's "sparkle." It's true, crystals do catch our eyes with their glitz and flash, and their enduring popularity gave us plenty of projects to choose from when we selected our favorite *Bead Style* crystal projects for inclusion in this volume of the *Simply Stylish* series.

But crystals have other appeal beyond their glimmer. They're incredibly versatile, pairing well with everything from liquid silver (Sue Godfrey's "Flash flood," p. 9) to WireLace (Linda Hartung's "Autumn leaves," p. 12) to chain (Liisa Turunen's "Sophisticated charm," p. 49). There's no denying the appeal of the wide variety of colors available. And thanks to the recent explosion in crystal shapes, you can work with barbell crystals (Jenna Colyar-Cooper's "Knockout earrings," p. 24), square crystals (Karla Schafer's "Stack of sparkle," p. 55), and teardrop-shaped crystals (Linda Hartung's "Stroke of genius," p. 25) — not to mention the perpetually popular rounds and bicones. The talented designers featured in this book present a wide array of styles and uses for these stunning little beads.

So just turn the page and let the versatility, the colors, the shapes — and, yes, the sparkle — of crystals inspire you as you create beautiful necklaces, bracelets, earrings, and rings with *Simply Stylish Crystal Jewelry*.

Basic Techniques

Cutting flexible beading wire
Decide how long you want your necklace to be. For a necklace, add 6 in. (15cm) and cut a piece of beading wire to that length. (For a bracelet, add 5 in./13cm.)

Cutting memory wire
Memory wire is hardened steel, so it will dent and ruin the jaws of most wire cutters. Use heavy-duty wire cutters or cutters specifically designed for memory wire, or bend the wire back and forth until it snaps.

Flattened crimp
1 Hold the crimp bead with the tip of your chainnose pliers. Squeeze the pliers firmly to flatten the crimp bead. Tug the clasp to make sure the crimp has a solid grip on the wire. If the wire slides, remove the crimp bead and repeat with a new crimp bead.

2 The flattened crimp.

Folded crimp
1 Position the crimp bead in the notch closest to the crimping pliers' handle.

2 Separate the wires and firmly squeeze the crimp bead.

3 Move the crimp bead into the notch at the pliers' tip. Squeeze the pliers, folding the bead in half at the indentation.

4 The folded crimp.

Crimp end

1 Glue one end of the cord and place it in a crimp end. Use chainnose pliers to fold one side of the crimp end over the cord.

2 Repeat with the second side of the crimp end and squeeze gently.

Opening a jump ring or loop

1 Hold the jump ring or loop with chainnose and roundnose pliers or two pairs of chainnose pliers.

2 To open the jump ring or loop, bring one pair of pliers toward you.

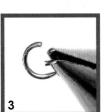

3 The open jump ring. Reverse the steps to close.

Attaching a clasp

1 For a two-piece clasp, on each end, string: spacer, crimp bead, spacer, Wire Guardian (optional), half of a clasp. Check the fit, and add or remove beads if necessary. Go back through the beads just strung and tighten the wire. Crimp the crimp bead and trim the excess wire.

2 Or, follow step 1 to attach a lobster claw clasp on one end and a soldered jump ring or chain extender on the other.

Overhand knot

Make a loop and pass the working end through it. Pull the ends to tighten the knot.

Surgeon's knot

Cross the right end over the left and go through the loop. Go through again. Cross the left end over the right and go through. Pull the ends to tighten the knot.

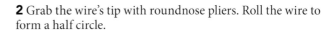
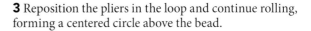

Plain loop

1 Trim the wire ⅜ in. (1cm) above the top bead. Make a right-angle bend close to the bead.

2 Grab the wire's tip with roundnose pliers. Roll the wire to form a half circle.

3 Reposition the pliers in the loop and continue rolling, forming a centered circle above the bead.

4 The finished loop.

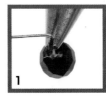

Wrapped loop

1 Make sure there is at least 1¼ in. (3.2cm) of wire above the bead. With the tip of your chainnose pliers, grasp the wire directly above the bead. Bend the wire (above the pliers) into a right angle.

2 Position the jaws of your roundnose pliers vertically in the bend.

3 Bring the wire over the pliers' top jaw.

4 Reposition the pliers' lower jaw snugly in the curved wire. Wrap the wire down and around the bottom of the pliers. This is "the first half of a wrapped loop."

Wrapped loop instructions continue on next page . . .

5 Grasp the loop with chainnose pliers.

6 Wrap the wire tail around the wire stem, covering the stem between the loop and the top bead. Trim the excess wrapping wire, and press the end close to the stem with chainnose or crimping pliers.

 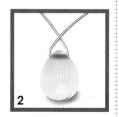

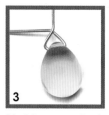 

Making a set of wraps above a top-drilled bead

1 Center a top-drilled bead on a 3-in. (7.6cm) piece of wire. Bend each end upward.

2 Cross the wires into an X.

3 Using chainnose pliers, make a small bend in each wire to form a right angle.

4 Wrap the horizontal wire around the vertical wire as in a wrapped loop. Trim the excess wrapping wire.

Split ring
Slide the hooked tip of a pair of split-ring pliers between the two overlapping wires.

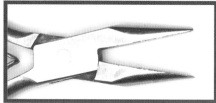

Chainnose pliers have smooth, flat inner jaws, and the tips taper to a point. Use them for gripping and for opening and closing loops and jump rings.

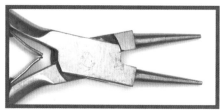

Roundnose pliers have smooth, tapered, conical jaws used to make loops. The closer to the tip you work, the smaller the loop will be.

Crimping pliers have two grooves in their jaws that are used to fold or roll a crimp bead into a compact shape.

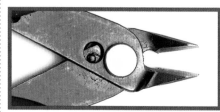

With **diagonal wire cutters**, use the front of the blades to make a pointed cut and the back of the blades to make a flat cut.

Use **split-ring pliers** to simplify opening split rings by inserting a curved jaw between the wires.

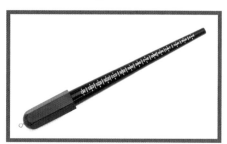

Twisted wire needles are made from a length of fine wire folded in half and twisted tightly together. They have a large open eye at the fold, which is easy to thread. The eye flattens when you pull the needles through the beads.

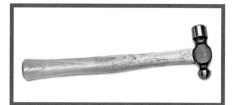

A **mandrel** is used to shape wire into uniform loops and angles, or to measure wire for rings, bracelets, or jewelry components. (Ring mandrel pictured.)

A **hammer** is used to harden wire. Any hammer with a flat head will work, as long as the head is free of nicks that could mar your metal. The light ball-peen hammer shown here is one of the most commonly used hammers for jewelry making.

A **bench block** provides a hard, smooth surface on which to hammer your pieces. An anvil is similarly hard but has different surfaces, such as a tapered horn, to help form wire into different shapes.

Materials

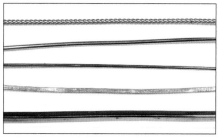

Clasps come in many sizes and shapes. Some of the most common are the toggle, consisting of a ring and a bar; lobster claw, which opens when you pull a tiny lever; S-hook, which links two soldered jump rings or split rings; hook-and-eye, consisting of a hook and a jump ring or split ring; and slide, consisting of one tube that slides inside another.

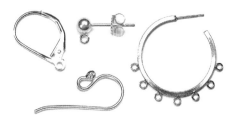

Earring findings come in a variety of metals and styles, including lever-back, post, hoop, and French hook. You will almost always want a loop (or loops) on earring findings so you can attach beads.

A **jump ring** is used to connect two components. It is a small wire circle or oval that is either soldered or comes with an opening. **Split rings** are used like jump rings but are much more secure. They look like tiny key rings and are made of springy wire.

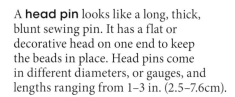

A **head pin** looks like a long, thick, blunt sewing pin. It has a flat or decorative head on one end to keep the beads in place. Head pins come in different diameters, or gauges, and lengths ranging from 1–3 in. (2.5–7.6cm).

Crimp beads and **tubes** are small, large-holed, thin-walled metal beads designed to be flattened or crimped into a tight roll. Use them when stringing jewelry on flexible beading wire. **Crimp bead covers** provide a way to hide your crimps by covering them with a finding that mimics the look of a small bead.

Crimp ends and **pinch ends** are used to connect the ends of leather, ribbons, or other fiber lacing materials to a clasp.

Findings like multi-strand spacer bars, connectors, spacers, filigree and chandelier components, tube beads, and cones let you connect and position the elements of your jewelry.

Flexible beading wire is composed of steel wires twisted together and covered with nylon. This wire is much stronger than thread and does not stretch; the higher the number of inner strands (between three and 49), the more flexible and kink-resistant the wire. It is available in a variety of sizes.

Wire is available in a number of materials and finishes, including brass, gold, gold-filled, gold-plated, fine silver, sterling silver, anodized niobium (chemically colored wire), and copper. Brass, copper, and craft wire are packaged in 10–40-yd. (9.5–36.6m) spools, while gold, silver, and niobium are usually sold by the foot or ounce. Wire thickness is measured by gauge — the higher the gauge, the thinner the wire — and is available in varying hardnesses and shapes, including twisted, round, half-round, and square.

Memory wire is steel spring wire; it's used for coiled bracelets, necklaces, and rings.

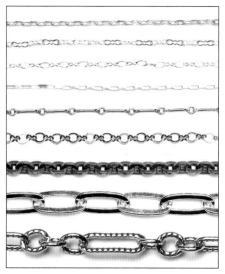

Chain is available in many finishes (sterling silver, gold-filled, base metal, plated metal) and styles (curb, figaro, long-and-short, rolo, cable). Often chain links can be opened in the same way loops and jump rings are opened.

Crystals & Glass

A BRIEF HISTORY OF CRYSTALS

1600s
Englishman George Ravenscroft discovers that adding lead oxide to molten glass increases the weight, clarity, and refraction of his glassware.

1700s
Crystals begin to be used in jewelry, often by the growing merchant class as they imitate the styles and trends of the upper class's gemstone jewelry. Upperclass ladies often have crystal (or "paste") copies of their jewels made so they can wear them without fear of theft.

1800s
Daniel Swarovski, the son of a Bohemian gem cutter, starts a crystal production business that soon garners a reputation for excellence. To protect the secrets of the manufacturing process and crystal-cutting machine he invented, Swarovski moves his business to the tiny village of Watten in rural Austria.

1900s
Crystals in some form remain present in fashion throughout the twentieth century, and Swarovki's reputation continues to grow as they partner with houses like Chanel, Dior, and Yves St. Laurent. They also expand their color and shape offerings, particularly at the end of the century as computer technology to aid in precision crystal cutting is developed.

BEADING WITH CRYSTALS

Crystal beads are made of the same materials that make up ordinary glass — sand, soda ash, and limestone — but have high lead oxide content. Most crystal beads have 10 to 35% lead oxide content. The lead-infused glass causes light to refract at a high level and gives crystals their trademark sparkle. Be sure that any crystals you use are free of abrasions, cuts, or flaws that may weaken your beading wire. The facets of the crystal should line up perfectly, and there should be no variation in shape or size from bead to bead. A variety of options are available for purchasing your crystals, but the best known are Swarovski, famous for their history, quality, and color, shape, and finish varieties.

SHAPES AND COLORS

Crystals can be found in familiar shapes like bicones and biolettes, as well as specialty shapes, like barbells, stars, flowers, leaves, buttons, daggers, and frames. Flatback crystals have one flat side for applying glue to attach the crystal to a clasp, pendant, bracelet form, or other item. Some crystals come pre-set, like channel-set or pre-made crystal webbing.

Crystals are available in a wide variety of finishes, like opaque or aurora borealis (AB), and colors, as well. In the projects that follow, the exact crystal choices of the designer were indicated if the color or finish was considered a key element of the design. If you encounter a project that doesn't indicate the crystal colors used and wish to know this information, contact information for the designers is located at the back of the book. Otherwise, we encourage you to creatively adapt and make each project your own with your personal color selections.

COMMONLY USED CRYSTAL SHAPES:

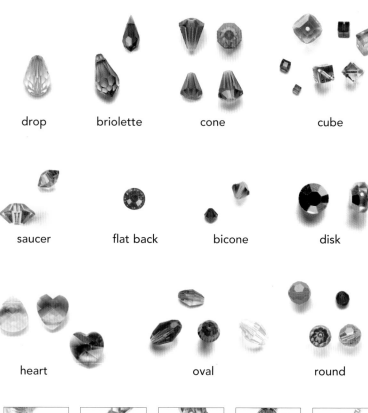

drop   briolette   cone   cube

saucer   flat back   bicone   disk

heart   oval   round

petal

leaf

channel set

barbell

frame

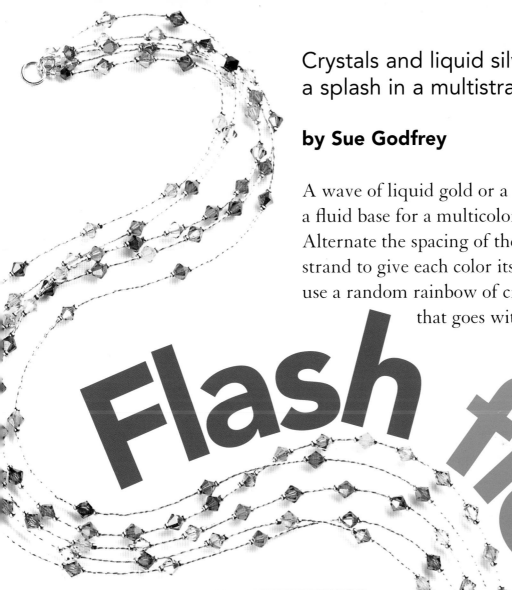

Crystals and liquid silver or gold make
a splash in a multistrand necklace

by Sue Godfrey

A wave of liquid gold or a current of silver offers
a fluid base for a multicolored crystal collection.
Alternate the spacing of the crystals on each
strand to give each color its chance to shine. Or,
use a random rainbow of crystals for a necklace
that goes with everything.

Flash flood

Supply**List**

both projects
- flexible beading wire, .014 or .015
- **10** crimp beads
- **2** 4mm soldered jump rings
- 4mm jump ring
- 4mm split ring
- lobster claw clasp
- chainnose pliers
- crimping pliers (optional)
- diagonal wire cutters
- roundnose pliers

gold necklace 17½ in. (44.5cm)
- **120–145** 4mm crystals
- 12g liquid-gold beads

silver rainbow necklace 17½ in.
- **130–150** 4mm crystals
- **10** 3mm bicone crystals
- 5g 13º seed beads
- 10g liquid-silver beads

9

COLOR NOTES
Swarovski Crystallized Elements

gold necklace
- **45–50** padparadscha bicones
- **25–30** Indian red rounds
- **20–25** light Colorado topaz AB rounds
- **15–20** Ceylon topaz bicones
- **15–20** light peach satin bicones

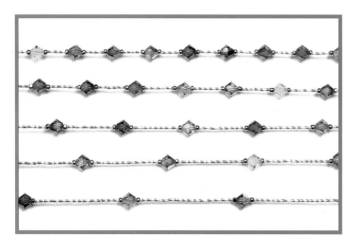

1 **silver rainbow necklace** • Cut five pieces of beading wire (Basics). Tape one end of each wire. On one wire, string two liquid-silver beads, a 13º seed bead, a 4mm bicone crystal, and a 13º. Repeat until the strand is within 1 in. (2.5cm) of the desired length, ending with two liquid-silver beads. Tape the end.

On the second wire, string three liquid-silver beads, a 13º, a 4mm bicone, and a 13º. Repeat until the strand is within 1 in. (2.5cm) of the desired length, ending with three liquid-silver beads. Tape the end.

On the third wire, string five liquid-silver beads, a 13º, a 4mm bicone, and a 13º. Repeat until the strand is within 1 in. (2.5cm) of the desired length, ending with five liquid-silver beads. Tape the end.

On the fourth wire, string seven liquid-silver beads, a 13º, a 4mm bicone, and a 13º. Repeat until the strand is within 1 in. (2.5cm) of the desired length, ending with seven liquid-silver beads. Tape the end.

On the fifth wire, string eight liquid-silver beads, a 13º, a 4mm bicone, and a 13º. Repeat until the strand is within 1 in. (2.5cm) of the desired length, ending with eight liquid-silver beads. Tape the end.

2 Arrange the strands as desired, with the longest strand on the bottom. Remove the tape from one end of a strand. String a 13º, a 3mm bicone, a crimp bead, a 13º, and a soldered jump ring. Go back through the last three beads and tighten the wire. Repeat with the remaining strands, attaching all the ends on each side to a single jump ring. Check the fit, and add or remove beads from each end if necessary. Crimp the crimp beads (Basics) and trim the excess wire.

3 Attach a split ring to one of the soldered jump rings. Open a jump ring (Basics) and attach a clasp to the other soldered jump ring. Close the jump ring.

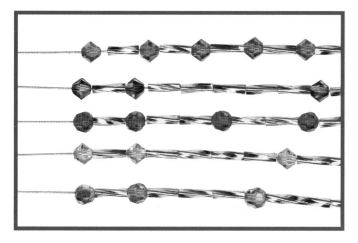

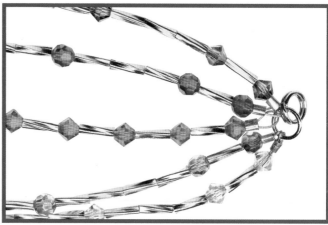

1 gold necklace • Cut five pieces of beading wire (Basics). On one wire, string a padparadscha crystal and a liquid-gold bead. Repeat until the strand is within 1 in. (2.5cm) of the desired length, ending with a crystal. Tape the ends.

On the second wire, string a light-peach-satin crystal and five gold beads. Repeat until the strand is within 1½ in. (3.8cm) of the desired length, ending with a crystal. String a gold bead and a crystal on each end. Tape the ends.

On the third wire, string an Indian-red crystal and two gold beads. Repeat until the strand is within 1½ in. of the desired length, ending with a crystal. String a gold bead and a crystal on each end. Tape the ends.

On the fourth wire, string a Ceylon-topaz crystal and four gold beads. Repeat until the strand is within 1½ in. of the desired length, ending with a crystal. String a gold bead and a crystal on each end. Tape the ends.

On the fifth wire, string a light-Colorado-topaz AB crystal and three gold beads. Repeat until the strand is within 1 in. of the desired length, ending with a crystal. String a gold bead and a crystal on each end. Tape the ends.

2 Arrange the strands with the longest strand on the bottom. Remove the tape from the end of one strand. String a crimp bead and a soldered jump ring. Go back through the last three beads and tighten the wire. Repeat on the other end. Repeat with the remaining strands, attaching all the ends on each side to a single jump ring. Check the fit, and add or remove beads from each end if necessary. Crimp the crimp beads (Basics) and trim the excess wire.

3 Attach a split ring to one of the soldered jump rings. Open a jump ring (Basics) and attach a clasp to the other soldered jump ring. Close the jump ring.

TIP
When using liquid silver or gold with a narrow (1mm) diameter, string 13º metallic seed beads next to the crystals. Otherwise, the "liquid" will flow into the crystals.

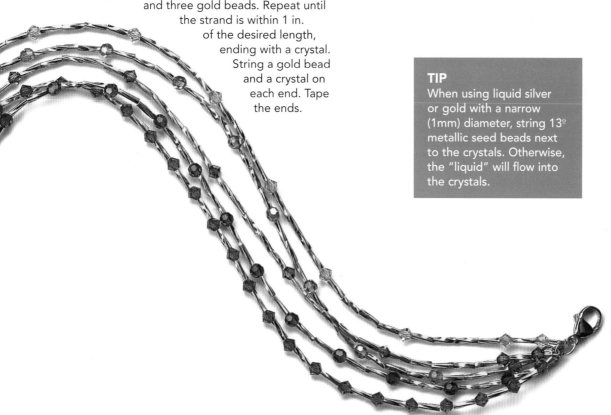

Autumn leaves

Crystals and WireLace play with fall light

by Linda Hartung

The vision of delicate autumn leaves stirred by this gorgeous bracelet-and-earrings set makes saying goodbye to summer a little less painful. While most sets revolve around a necklace, this bracelet is complex enough to stand on its own.

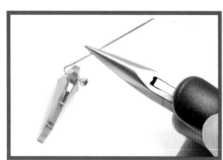

1 **bracelet** • On a crystal-studded head pin, string a leaf-shaped crystal. Bend the head pin back over the top of the leaf at a 45-degree angle.

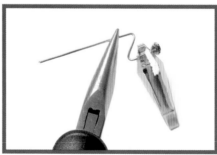

2 About ¼ in. (6mm) from the first bend, bend the wire away from the leaf at a 45-degree angle.

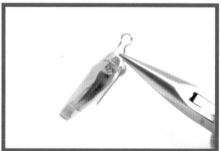

3 Use roundnose pliers to grip the head pin at the second bend. Wrap the wire around the jaws of your roundnose pliers to make half of a loop. Make three half-wrapped leaf units.

4 On a head pin, string a 4mm bicone crystal, a 6mm bicone crystal, and an 8mm bicone crystal. Make the first half of a wrapped loop (Basics). Make 12 bicone units, completing the wraps on two of the units.

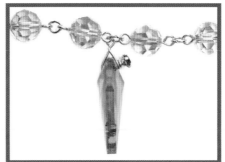

5 Cut a piece of chain with 11 crystal units, leaving a link on each end. Attach a leaf unit to every third link. Wrap the head pins as shown and trim the excess wire.

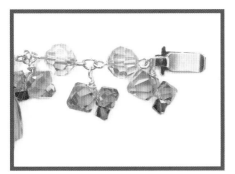

6 Attach a half-wrapped bicone unit to each link between the crystal links. Complete the wraps. On each end, open the link and attach a wrapped bicone unit and half of a clasp. Close the link.

7 Cut a 10-in. (25cm) piece of Wire-Lace. String an end link of the chain and tie two overhand knots (Basics) around the link.

8 Weave the lace through each link, tying overhand knots next to each bicone unit as you go. Insert your finger between the chain and the lace as you tie knots, creating loops. Apply two-part epoxy to the end knots and trim the excess lace.

9 Gently pull apart the WireLace loops to create waves.

SupplyList

bracelet 7¾ in. (19.7cm)
- **3** 26mm leaf-shaped crystals
- **12** 8mm bicone crystals, top-drilled
- **12** 6mm bicone crystals, top-drilled
- **12** 4mm bicone crystals
- **10** in. (25cm) 6mm WireLace
- **7** in. (18cm) crystal chain
- **3** 1½-in. (3.8cm) crystal-studded head pins
- **12** 2-in. (5cm) head pins
- leaf clasp
- chainnose pliers
- diagonal wire cutters
- roundnose pliers
- two-part epoxy

earrings
- **2** 26mm leaf-shaped crystals
- **2** 8mm bicone crystals, top-drilled
- **4** 6mm bicone crystals, top-drilled
- **2** 4mm bicone crystals
- **2** 1½-in. (3.8cm) crystal-studded head pins
- **2** 2-in. (5cm) head pins
- **2** 4mm jump rings
- pair of cup-and-post earrings with ear nuts
- chainnose pliers
- diagonal wire cutters
- roundnose pliers
- two-part epoxy

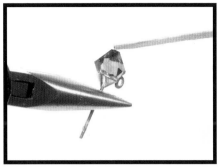

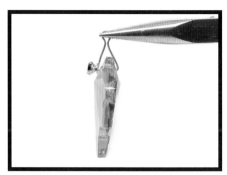

1 **earrings** • Apply two-part epoxy to the cup of an earring post. Insert the hole end of a 6mm top-drilled bicone in the cup.

2 Following bracelet steps 1 to 3, make a leaf unit. Complete the wraps.

3 On a head pin, string a 4mm bicone crystal, a 6mm bicone crystal, and an 8mm bicone crystal. Make a wrapped loop (Basics).

4 Open a jump ring (Basics). Attach the leaf unit, the bicone unit, and the loop of the earring post. Close the jump ring. Make a second earring to match the first.

DESIGN ALTERNATIVE
Replace the leaf-shaped crystals with filigree foliage to match the delicacy of the WireLace.

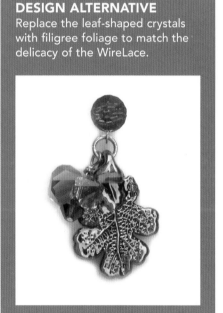

TIP
Despite the number of steps, the techniques used in this project are relatively simple. If you plan to make both pieces, keep things organized by making the leaf and bicone dangles all at once.

Colors of
the prairie

A jewelry set evokes memories of Circle City

by Katie Hacker

Katie was inspired to design this necklace and bracelet while pondering the view from her Keystone, Indiana, home. "The colors remind me of the grass and wheat below a summer sky," she says. "And Indianapolis was once called Circle City, so this set has a fun connection to my birthplace, too."

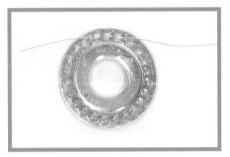

1 necklace • Cut a 4-in. (10cm) piece of beading wire. String 23 4mm helix crystals. String one end through the beads in the opposite direction, pulling the ends to form a circle. Place the circle in the outside channel of a double-circle component.

2 Cut a 3-in. (7.6cm) piece of wire. String 14 4mm round crystals. Make a circle of beads as in step 1. Place the circle in the inside channel of the double-circle component.

3 On a decorative head pin, string an 8 mm helix crystal. String the holes of the circle component, making sure the head pin is on top of the wires. Make a wrapped loop (Basics). Trim the wire tails. Cut a 12-in. (30 cm) piece of beading wire. Center the pendant.

4 On a decorative head pin, string a crystal. Make a wrapped loop. Make 12 6mm helix units, 12 6mm round units, 12 6mm rondelle units, and 24 4mm round units.

5 On each end of the wire, string: round pearl, 4mm round unit, 6mm helix unit, 6mm round unit, 6mm rondelle unit, 4mm round unit. Repeat five times.

TIPS

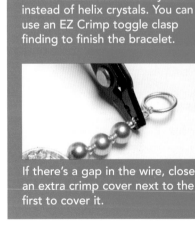

Make sure you use 4mm crystals to fill the circle components. Slightly larger crystals will not fit. You can also use round crystals instead of helix crystals. You can use an EZ Crimp toggle clasp finding to finish the bracelet.

If there's a gap in the wire, close an extra crimp cover next to the first to cover it.

6 Cut two 6–8-in. (15–20cm) pieces of chain. On each end of the beaded strand, string a crimp bead and a chain. Go back through the last few beads strung and tighten the wire. Crimp the crimp bead (Basics) and trim the excess wire.

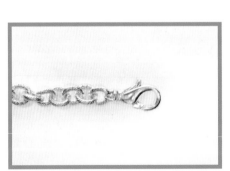

7 Close a crimp cover over each crimp. On one end of the chain, open a link (Basics) and attach a lobster claw clasp. Close the link.

SupplyList

necklace 17 in. (43cm)
- 35mm Katiedids double-circle component (katiehacker.com)
- 8mm helix crystal
- **12** 6mm helix crystals
- **23** 4mm helix crystals
- **12** 6mm crystal rondelles
- **12** 6mm round crystals
- **38** 4mm round crystals
- **12** 6mm round pearls

- flexible beading wire, .014 or .015
- 12–16 in. (30–41cm) chain, 5–7mm links
- **61** 2-in. (5cm) decorative head pins
- **2** crimp beads
- **2** crimp covers
- lobster claw clasp
- chainnose pliers
- crimping pliers
- diagonal wire cutters
- roundnose pliers

bracelet 7¼ in. (18.4cm)
- **3** 25mm Katiedids single-circle components
- **8–12** 8mm round pearls
- **3** 8mm helix crystals, in **3** colors
- **14** 4mm helix crystals
- **28** 4mm round crystals, in **2** colors
- **10–14** 5mm spacers

- flexible beading wire, .014 or .015
- **2** crimp beads
- **2–4** crimp covers
- toggle clasp
- crimping pliers
- diagonal wire cutters

1 bracelet • Following step 2 of the necklace, make a circle of 4mm round crystals. Place the circle in the channel of a single-circle component. Make another round-crystal component and a 4mm helix-crystal component. Cut a piece of beading wire (Basics). Center: round pearl, hole of the helix-crystal component, spacer, 8mm helix crystal, spacer, second hole of the component, pearl.

2 On each end, string: hole of a round-crystal component, spacer, 8mm helix crystal, spacer, second hole of the component. String alternating pearls and spacers until the strand is within 1 in. (2.5cm) of the finished length.

3 On each end, attach half of a toggle clasp (Basics). Close a crimp cover over each crimp.

Glitzy links

Foil-backed crystal buttons provide depth and sparkle

by Patricia Bartlein

Decorative jump rings offer a handy way to turn these buttons into jewelry. To match their intensity, combine them with bicones in "shadow" for dazzling earrings.

1 bracelet • Open a jump ring (Basics). String three jump rings and one hole of a crystal button. Close the jump ring.

2 Use a jump ring to attach the set of three jump rings and one hole of a button.

3 Repeat steps 1 and 2 until the bracelet is within 1 in. (2.5cm) of the finished length, ending with three jump rings on each end. Check the fit, and add or remove jump rings or buttons if necessary.

4 On each end, use a jump ring to attach half of a clasp.

5 On a head pin, string a 4mm bicone crystal, a 6mm bicone crystal, and a 4mm bicone. Make a plain loop (Basics). Make a one-bicone unit and a two-bicone unit as shown.

6 Use a jump ring to attach the three bicone units and an end jump ring.

SupplyList

bracelet 7¼ in. (18.4cm)
- **7–8** 12mm square crystal buttons
- **3** 6mm bicone crystals
- **3** 4mm bicone crystals
- **3** 1½-in. (3.8cm) 22-gauge head pins
- **41–46** 7mm decorative jump rings
- toggle clasp
- chainnose pliers
- diagonal wire cutters
- roundnose pliers

earrings
- **2** 12mm square crystal buttons
- **4** 6mm bicone crystals
- **2** 4mm bicone crystals
- **2** 2 in. (5cm) 22-gauge half-hard wire
- **2** 1½-in. (3.8cm) 22-gauge head pins
- **4** 7mm decorative jump rings
- pair of earring wires
- chainnose pliers
- diagonal wire cutters
- roundnose pliers

TIP
To alter the length of the bracelet just a little, use 4mm jump rings to attach the clasp.

1 earrings • On a head pin, string a 4mm bicone crystal and a 6mm bicone crystal. Make a plain loop (Basics).

Cut a 1-in. (2.5cm) piece of wire. Make a plain loop. String a 6mm bicone and make a plain loop.

2 Open a jump ring (Basics). Attach the head pin unit and one hole of a crystal button. Close the jump ring. Use a jump ring to attach one loop of the remaining bicone unit and the remaining button hole.

3 Open the loop of an earring wire (Basics). Attach the dangle and close the loop. Make a second earring to match the first.

String a splash of crystals

Go glamorous with a high-gleam necklace and earrings

by Irina Miech

Mix a trio of crystal shapes with silver accents to create jewelry that reflects elegance with every facet. Keeping the colors in the same family creates a subtle glow.

SupplyList

necklace 16½ in. (41.9cm)
- **3** 16mm pear-shaped crystals
- **2** 11mm pear-shaped crystals
- **100–110** 4mm round crystals
- **100–110** 3mm bicone crystals
- **120–140** 2mm round spacers
- flexible beading wire, .014 or .015
- **2** in. (5cm) chain, 5–7mm links
- **65** 2-in. (5cm) head pins
- **2** crimp beads
- lobster claw clasp
- chainnose pliers
- crimping pliers (optional)
- diagonal wire cutters
- roundnose pliers

earrings
- **2** 11mm pear-shaped crystals
- **20–26** 3mm bicone crystals
- **18–24** 2mm round spacers
- **18–24** 2-in. (5cm) head pins
- **8** in. (20cm) 24-gauge half-hard wire
- pair of earring wires
- chainnose pliers
- diagonal wire cutters
- roundnose pliers

1 necklace • On a head pin, string a bicone crystal, a round crystal, and a spacer. Make a wrapped loop (Basics). Make a total of 64 crystal units.

2 Cut a piece of beading wire (Basics). Center a 16mm pear-shaped crystal on the wire.

3 On each end, string 16 crystal units and a 16mm pear-shaped crystal.

4 On each end, string 16 crystal units and an 11mm pear-shaped crystal.

COLOR NOTES
Swarovski Crystallized Elements

light crystal set
   pear-shaped crystals: crystal AB
   4mm round crystals: white opal
   3mm bicone crystals: pacific opal

dark crystal set
   pear-shaped crystals: aquamarine
   4mm round crystals: aquamarine
   3mm bicone crystals: indicolite

5 On each end, string a spacer, a round crystal, a spacer, and a bicone. Repeat until the strand is within ½ in. (1.3cm) of the finished length. End with a spacer.

6 On a head pin, string a bicone, a round crystal, and a spacer. Make the first half of a wrapped loop. Cut a 2-in. (5cm) piece of chain. Attach the crystal unit and complete the wraps.

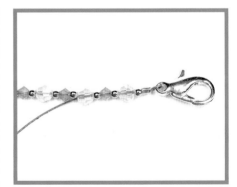

7 On one end, string a crimp bead and a lobster claw clasp. Repeat on the other end, substituting the chain for the clasp.

Check the fit, and finish the necklace (Basics).

1 earrings • On a head pin, string a bicone crystal and a round spacer. Make a wrapped loop (Basics). Make a total of nine to 12 crystal units.

2 Cut a 4-in. (10cm) piece of wire. String an 11mm pear-shaped crystal and make a set of wraps above it (Basics).

String a bicone. With the largest part of your roundnose pliers, make the first half of a wrapped loop.

3 Attach the crystal units to the wrapped loop. Complete the wraps.

4 Open the loop of an earring wire (Basics). Attach the dangle and close the loop. Make a second earring to match the first.

DESIGN ALTERNATIVE
Replace the crystal strand with a silver chain to draw more attention to the sparkling centerpiece.

Knockout earrings

Barbell-shaped crystals give earrings some fashion muscle

by Jenna Colyar-Cooper

For a pair of fabulous earrings, barbell-shaped crystals and jump rings make a winning combination. Pick contrasting crystal colors for a high-impact design. In 15 minutes, you'll have modern earrings that pack a style punch.

1 Open a jump ring (Basics). String a color A barbell-shaped crystal and close the jump ring.

2 Open another jump ring. String a color B barbell and attach the previous jump ring. Close the jump ring. Use jump rings to attach a color A, color B, and color A barbell.

3 Open the loop of an earring wire (Basics). Attach the dangle and close the loop. Make a second earring to match the first.

Supply List

earrings
- **10** 11mm barbell-shaped crystals, **6** in color A, **4** in color B
- **10** 7.3mm jump rings
- pair of earring wires
- chainnose and roundnose pliers, or **2** pairs of chainnose pliers

DESIGN ALTERNATIVE
For sleeker baubles, try long earrings with a single color. Each earring shown here uses 12 crystal-colored barbells.

Stroke of genius

Brushstroke-shaped crystals inspire design

by Linda Hartung

As soon as Linda saw the curves of these crystals, she thought of the brushwork of impressionists such as Monet, Renoir, and Degas. The brushstroke-shaped crystals (Swarovski Crystallized Elements calls them aquiline) come top- or center-drilled, but the options aren't available in all colors and sizes. The trick is to organize your shopping: Check availability, plan the jewelry bead by bead, make a list, and then shop.

ASSEMBLING A CLASP
- 8mm crystal teardrop flat back Swarovski #4300
- **2** 8mm crystal oval flat backs or navettes Swarovski #4200
- **2** 5mm crystal flat back rhinestones Swarovski #1028
- two-part epoxy
- tweezers or a toothpick with a bit of museum putty

Apply two-part epoxy to the inside of each bezel. Set the crystal, making sure it is level. Let dry.

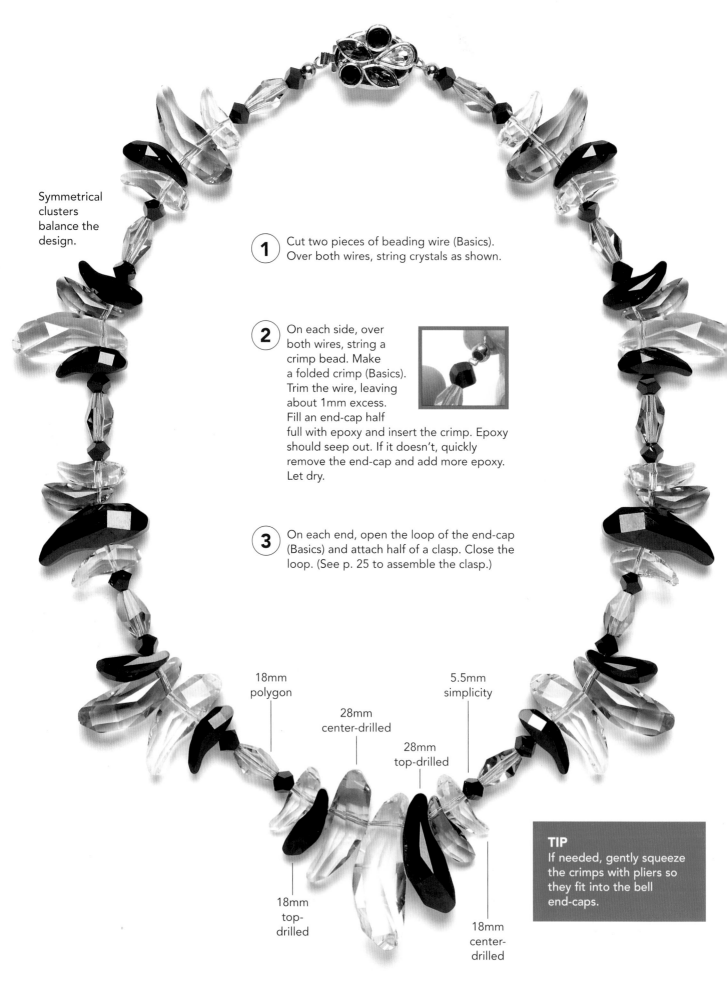

Symmetrical clusters balance the design.

1 Cut two pieces of beading wire (Basics). Over both wires, string crystals as shown.

2 On each side, over both wires, string a crimp bead. Make a folded crimp (Basics). Trim the wire, leaving about 1mm excess. Fill an end-cap half full with epoxy and insert the crimp. Epoxy should seep out. If it doesn't, quickly remove the end-cap and add more epoxy. Let dry.

3 On each end, open the loop of the end-cap (Basics) and attach half of a clasp. Close the loop. (See p. 25 to assemble the clasp.)

18mm polygon

5.5mm simplicity

28mm center-drilled

28mm top-drilled

18mm top-drilled

18mm center-drilled

TIP
If needed, gently squeeze the crimps with pliers so they fit into the bell end-caps.

SupplyList

necklace 19 in. (48cm)
- 36mm aquiline crystal, top drilled, color A
- **5** 28mm aquiline crystals, top drilled, **2** color A, **2** color B, **1** color C
- **7** 28mm aquiline crystals, center drilled, **2** color A, **3** color B, **2** color C
- **10** 18mm aquiline crystals, top drilled, **5** color B, **5** color C
- **16** 18mm aquiline crystals, center drilled, **10** color A, **6** color C
- **10** 18mm polygon crystals, color A
- **20** 5.5mm simplicity crystals, color C
- flexible beading wire, .018 or .019
- **2** crimp beads
- **2** 4mm bell end-caps
- box clasp
- chainnose and roundnose pliers, or **2** pairs of chainnose pliers
- crimping pliers
- diagonal wire cutters
- two-part epoxy

bracelet 7 in. (18cm)
- **12** 18mm aquiline crystals, top drilled, **3** color A, **6** color B, **3** color C
- **12** 18mm aquiline crystals, center drilled, **6** color A, **6** color C
- **7** 5.5mm simplicity crystals, color C
- flexible beading wire, .018 or .019
- **2** crimp beads
- **2** 4mm bell end-caps
- box clasp
- chainnose and roundnose pliers, or **2** pairs of chainnose pliers
- crimping pliers
- diagonal wire cutters
- two-part epoxy

TIPS
- One strand of .024 beading wire can be substituted for two strands of .018 or .019.
- Don't substitute bicones for the simplicity crystals. You'll lose the snug fit the simplicity shape gives.

COLOR NOTES
Swarovski Crystallized Elements

black and white
Color A: crystal
Color B: black diamond
Color C: jet

blue and green
Color A: crystal
Color B: aquamarine
Color C: olivine

DESIGN ALTERNATIVE
Knot and braid four coordinating strands of WireLace for a look that requires fewer crystals.

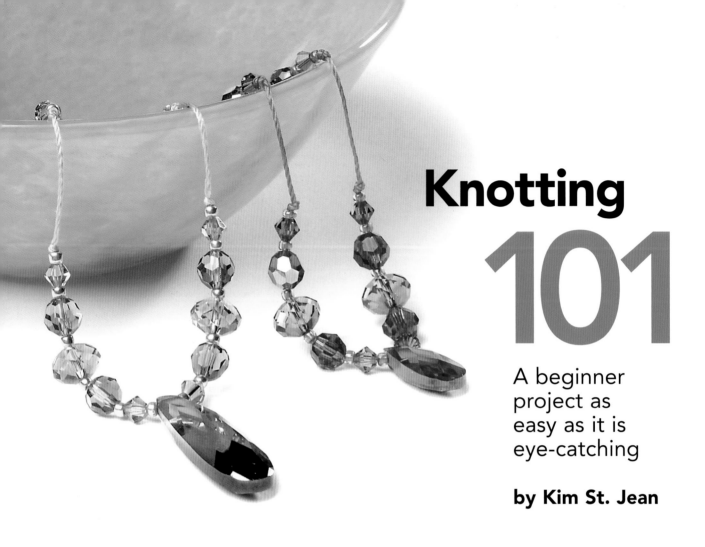

Knotting
101

A beginner project as easy as it is eye-catching

by Kim St. Jean

If you want a novice knotting project, this is the one for you. It looks great and is simple to build around the sleek shape of a CZ drop. This necklace and earrings garner so much attention, you'll find yourself making them in lots of color combinations.

1 necklace • Cut an 18–24-in. (46–61cm) piece of thread or braiding string. Center a pendant.

2 On each end, string: 11º seed bead, bicone crystal, 11º, round crystal, 11º, crystal rondelle, 11º, round, 11º, bicone, 11º. Tie an overhand knot (Basics) next to the last 11º.

3 a On each side, about 1 in. (2.5cm) from the knot, tie an overhand knot.
  b Repeat steps 2 and 3a until the necklace is within 1 in. (2.5cm) of the finished length.

4 Check the fit and trim the excess thread. Apply glue and string a crimp end. Flatten the crimp portion of the crimp end (Basics).
  Open a jump ring (Basics). Attach a lobster claw clasp and a crimp end. Close the jump ring. Repeat on the other end, substituting a chain for the clasp.

1 **earrings** • Cut a 6-in. (15cm) piece of thread or braiding string. String: 11º seed bead, bicone crystal, 11º, round crystal, 11º, crystal rondelle, 11º, round, 11º, bicone, 11º. Center the beads.

2 Tie an overhand knot (Basics) next to the first and last 11º.

3 Bring the ends together and trim to the desired length. Apply glue and string a crimp end over both ends. Flatten the crimp portion of the crimp end (Basics).

4 Open the loop of an earring wire (Basics) and attach the dangle. Close the loop. Make a second earring to match the first.

Supply List

necklace 19 in. (48cm)

- 18–36mm cubic zirconia (CZ) pendant
- **8–12** 8mm crystal rondelles
- **16–24** 6mm round crystals
- **16–24** 4mm bicone crystals
- 2g 11º seed beads
- 18–24 in. (46–61cm) C-Lon thread or braiding string
- **2** 4–6mm jump rings
- **2** crimp ends
- lobster claw clasp
- 2 in. (5cm) chain for extender, 2–3mm links
- chainnose and roundnose pliers, or **2** pairs of chainnose pliers
- diagonal wire cutters
- Bead Fix adhesive

earrings

- **2** 8mm crystal rondelles
- **4** 6mm round crystals
- **4** 4mm bicone crystals
- **12** 11º seed beads
- 12 in. (30cm) C-lon thread or braiding string
- **2** crimp ends
- pair of earring wires
- chainnose and roundnose pliers, or **2** pairs of chainnose pliers
- diagonal wire cutters
- Bead Fix adhesive

TIP
Use the tip of your roundnose pliers to push the beads together as you tighten each knot.

DESIGN ALTERNATIVE
For a more earthy option, try a neutral-toned gemstone pendant in place of the CZ pendant.

Delicate balance

Airy earrings represent heavenly bodies and natural laws

by Rachel Nelson-Smith

Multi-armed Shiva is one of the most complex Hindu deities, representing a multitude of qualities: destruction and restoration, asceticism and sensuality. Shape and bend sparkling arms of crystals and wire to create these challenging earrings in your own version of harmony.

SupplyList

earrings
- **8** 7–9mm crystal drops, vertically drilled
- **2** 8mm bicone crystals
- **24** 4mm bicone crystals in **2** colors:
  14 color A, **10** color B
- **8** 3mm round crystals
- **6** 1½-in. (3.8cm) 26-gauge head pins
- **4.5** ft. (1.4m) 26-gauge dead-soft wire
- pair of kidney or French earring wires
- chainnose pliers
- diagonal wire cutters
- roundnose pliers

1 String a 3mm round crystal on a head pin. Make a wrapped loop (Basics) above the crystal. Cut a 2½-in. (6.4cm) piece of wire. Make the first half of a wrapped loop at one end. Attach the crystal dangle and complete the wraps.

2 String a crystal drop and a color A 4mm bicone crystal. Make a wrapped loop above the top bicone. Repeat steps 1 and 2 to make a total of three drop units. Set two drop units aside for step 5.

3 Cut a 2-in. (5cm) piece of wire. Make the first half of a wrapped loop at one end. Attach a drop unit and complete the wraps. String a round crystal and make a wrapped loop.

4 Cut an 18-in. (46cm) piece of wire. Make the first half of a wrapped loop at the center. Attach the drop unit from step 3, and twist the wires several times.

5 On each side, approximately ½ in. (1.3cm) from the center loop, make the first half of a wrapped loop. Attach a drop unit from step 2 to each loop, and twist the wires together several times.

6 On each side, approximately ¼ in. (6mm) from the last twist, string a color B 4mm bicone crystal. Bend the wire around the bicone, and twist the wires together several times.

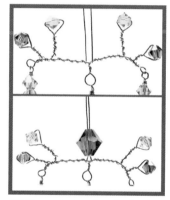

7 Repeat step 6, substituting an A 4mm bicone for the B 4mm bicone. Twist the wires until they meet above the center drop unit.

String an 8mm bicone crystal over both wires.

8 On each side, approximately ¼ in. (6mm) from the 8mm bicone, string a B bicone. Bend the wire around the bicone, and twist the wires together several times.

Approximately ¼ in. (6mm) from the last twist, repeat, substituting an A bicone for the B bicone. Twist the wires until they meet above the 8mm bicone.

9 String a crystal drop and a B bicone. Make a wrapped loop above the bicone with both wires.

10 Open the loop (Basics) of an earring wire and attach the dangle. Close the loop. Make a second earring to match the first.

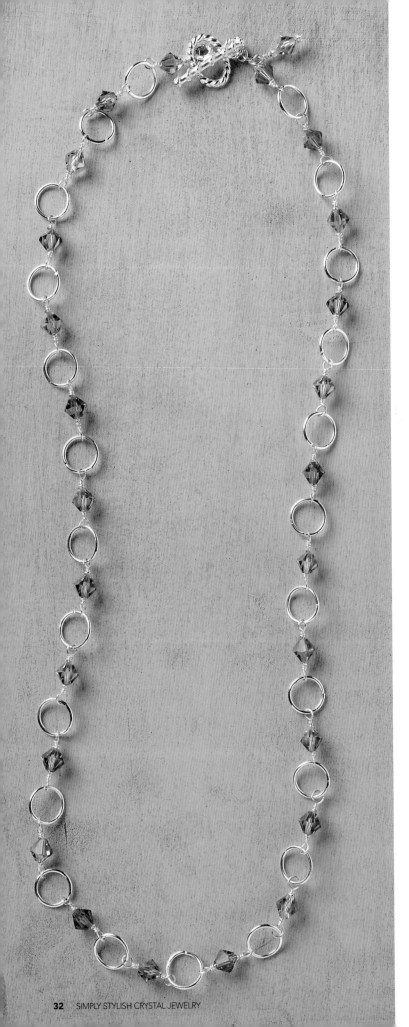

A modern take on blue

Simple elements shine in a contemporary necklace, bracelet, and earrings

by Jennifer Ortiz

For a sleek geometric necklace, link bicone crystals and jump rings. You'll be making lots of wrapped loops, so practice with inexpensive copper wire and refer to the Basic Techniques section if you need a quick refresher.

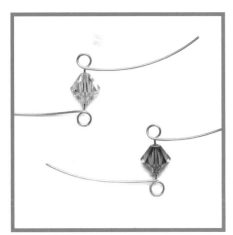

1 necklace • Cut a 3-in. (7.6cm) piece of wire. Make the first half of a wrapped loop (Basics) on one end. String a bicone crystal and make the first half of a wrapped loop. Make 25 to 29 bead units, in two colors.

2 Attach one loop of a bead unit to a soldered jump ring. Attach one loop of another bead unit to the jump ring. Attach a soldered jump ring to one loop. Complete the wraps as you go, leaving the first loop unwrapped. Continue attaching bead units and soldered jump rings until the necklace is within 1 in. (2.5cm) of the finished length, ending with an unwrapped loop.

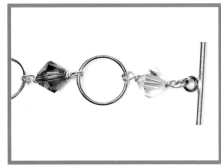

3 Check the fit, and add or remove bead units or jump rings if necessary. Complete the wraps on the end loops.

On each end, open a 3–4mm jump ring (Basics). Attach the end loop and half of a clasp. Close the jump ring.

4 On a head pin, string a spacer, a bicone, and a spacer. Make a wrapped loop.

DESIGN ALTERNATIVE
For an organic-looking necklace, use hammered jump rings. Simply place a soldered jump ring on a bench block or anvil, and hammer gently on both sides.

5 Use a 3–4mm jump ring to attach the bead unit to one of the end loops.

33

bracelet • Follow step 1 of the necklace, making eight or nine bead units. Follow steps 2–5.

1 **earrings •** On a head pin, string a spacer, a bicone crystal, and a spacer. Make the first half of a wrapped loop.

2 Cut a 3-in. (7.6cm) piece of wire. Make the first half of a wrapped loop (Basics) on one end. String a bicone and make the first half of a wrapped loop perpendicular to the first loop.

3 Attach the head pin unit to a soldered jump ring. Attach one loop of the remaining bead unit to the jump ring. Complete the wraps.

4 Open the loop of an earring wire (Basics). Attach the dangle and close the loop. Make a second earring to match the first.

Supply List

necklace 19¼ in. (48.9cm)
- **26–30** 6mm bicone crystals, in **2** colors
- **2** 2mm spacers
- **75–87** in. (1.9–2.2m) 24-gauge half-hard wire
- **1½-in.** (3.8cm) head pin
- **22–28** 10mm soldered jump rings
- **3** 3–4mm jump rings
- toggle clasp
- chainnose pliers
- diagonal wire cutters
- roundnose pliers

bracelet 7 in. (18cm)
- **9–11** 6mm bicone crystals, in **2** colors
- **2** 2mm spacers
- **24–30** in. (61–76cm) 24-gauge half-hard wire
- **1½-in.** (3.8cm) head pin
- **7–9** 10mm soldered jump rings
- **3** 3–4mm jump rings
- toggle clasp
- chainnose pliers
- diagonal wire cutters
- roundnose pliers

earrings
- **4** 6mm bicone crystals, in **2** colors
- **4** 2mm spacers
- **6** in. (15cm) 24-gauge half-hard wire
- **2** 1½-in. (3.8cm) head pins
- **2** 10mm soldered jump rings
- pair of earring wires
- chainnose pliers
- diagonal wire cutters
- roundnose pliers

Lush look

Get the rich look of rubies without the price tag

by Irina Miech

Faceted glass rondelles and crystal bicones in a palette of reds and blushes mimic regal rubies. Two-loop spacers give this bracelet an extra bit of swing as well as eye-catching glints of gold.

Supply List

bracelet 7¾ in. (19.7cm)
- **27–29** 7mm faceted glass rondelles
- **52–56** 4mm bicone crystals
- **26–28** 11mm two-loop spacers
- flexible beading wire, .014 or .015
- **52–56** 1½-in. (3.8cm) head pins
- **2** crimp beads
- toggle clasp
- chainnose pliers
- crimping pliers (optional)
- diagonal wire cutters
- roundnose pliers

TIP
Start with neutral-colored rondelles and use up the stray bicones in your stash for a multicolored version.

1 On a head pin, string a bicone crystal. Make a plain loop (Basics). Make 52 to 56 bicone units.

2 Open the loops of two bicone units (Basics) and attach the loops of a two-loop spacer. Close the loops. Make 26 to 28 spacer units.

3 Cut a piece of beading wire (Basics) and string a rondelle and a spacer unit. String an alternating pattern of rondelles and spacer units until the strand is within 1 in. (2.5cm) of the finished length. End with a rondelle.

4 On each end, string a crimp bead and half of a clasp. Check the fit, and finish the bracelet (Basics).

Crystal frame lariat

A sparkling lariat requires only two kinds of crystals

by Catherine Hodge

This monochromatic lariat is gorgeous with a cool palette, but you can dress your version up or down by trying different combinations of chain and crystals. Because it's so quick and easy to make, this lariat is perfect as an accessory — or a gift.

1 On a head pin, string a round crystal. Make the first half of a wrapped loop (Basics). Make 15 crystal units.

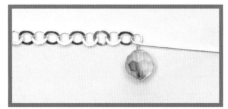

2 Decide how long you want your lariat to be and cut a piece of chain to that length. On one end, attach a crystal unit. Complete the wraps.

3 Attach a crystal unit to each adjacent link, completing the wraps as you go.

SupplyList

lariat 23 in. (58cm)
- 20mm square crystal ring
- **15** 6mm round crystals
- 22–26 in. (56–66cm) chain, 3mm links
- **15** 1½-in. (3.8cm) head pins
- 9–10mm jump ring
- chainnose pliers
- diagonal wire cutters
- roundnose pliers

DESIGN ALTERNATIVE
For a colorful option, use round crystals in a variety of shades. You can also use a different ring shape (like this a 22mm oval); just make sure the opening accommodates the cluster of 6mm crystals.

4 Open a jump ring (Basics) and attach a square ring and the other end of the chain. Close the jump ring.

Vintage

Sparkling crystals and luminescent pearls
dazzle in a four-strand necklace

vogue

by Lauren Branca

With crystals reminiscent of a vintage chandelier, this
striking necklace makes a bold statement. The three top
strands graduate a half inch in length, lending a subtle
drape to the choker portion of the piece. The longer
strand boasts a faceted crystal pendant, adding a
surprisingly modern twist to the choker. Try classic
white pearls or pale, muted shades and create your
own future heirloom.

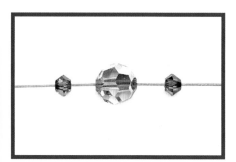

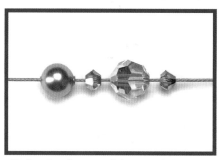

1 Cut four pieces of beading wire (Basics) to varying lengths. On the shortest wire, center a bicone, a round crystal, and a bicone.

2a On each end, string three pearls, a bicone, a round crystal, and a bicone. Repeat until the strand is within 1 in. (2.5cm) of the desired length. Tape the ends.

　b On the second longest (the third) wire, center the pattern in step 1. Then, repeat the pattern in step 2a until the strand is within 1 in. of the desired length. Tape the ends.

3 On the shorter of the remaining wires, center the pattern in step 1. On each end, string a pearl, a bicone, a round crystal, and a bicone. Repeat this pattern on each end until the strand is within 1 in. of the desired length. Tape the ends.

SupplyList

necklace,
longest strand 17½ in. (35.6cm)

• crystal pendant (the drop is
  31 x 50mm; the round is 40mm)
• 2 20-in. (51cm) strands 5mm
  round Swarovski pearls
• **60–70** 6mm round crystals
• 4mm accent crystal (optional)
• **120–140** 3mm bicone crystals
• flexible beading wire, .014 or .015
• 4 in. (10cm) 22-gauge
  half-hard wire
• **16** 3mm round spacers
• **8** crimp beads
• four-strand clasp
• chainnose pliers
• diagonal wire cutters
• crimping pliers (optional)
• roundnose pliers

TIP
Use man-made pearls for this
project. Their consistent size will
ensure an accurate pattern and fit.

4 String the pendant on the 22-gauge
wire 1½ in. (3.8cm) from one end
and bend each wire upward around the
pendant, as in wrapping above a top-
drilled bead (Basics). Wrap the shorter
wire around the longer wire and trim
the excess.

5 String a 4mm or 6mm crystal
and make a wrapped loop (Basics)
above the bead.

6 On the remaining wire, center a
bicone, the pendant, and a bicone.

7 On each end, string five pearls, a bicone, a round crystal,
and a bicone. Repeat until the strand is within 1 in. of the
desired length. Tape the ends.

8 Remove the tape from one end of each strand. On one
end of each strand, string a round spacer, a crimp bead,
a spacer, and the respective loop on half the clasp. Go back
through the last beads strung and tighten the wires. Repeat
on the other end. Check the fit, and add or remove an equal
number of beads from each end if necessary. Crimp the crimp
beads (Basics) and trim the excess wire.

COLOR NOTES
Swarovski Crystallized Elements

necklace
    polygon pendants:
        crystal golden shadow
        light azore
    6mm bicones:
        crystal golden shadow
    4mm bicones:
        Pacific opal
        light azore

Make a sparkling necklace
and earrings that celebrate
summer's beauty

by Suzanne Walters

CRYSTAL
sand & surf

Before moving to Colorado, Suzanne spent her life in Huntington Beach, California. The pale blue water and golden sand inspired this necklace and earrings. The jewelry is simple and light, yet the detail — wrapping all of the crystals — makes it special. If you opt for a set in different colors, start by selecting the polygon pendants, since they are available in fewer colors than the bicones.

1 necklace • On a head pin, string a 4mm bicone crystal. Make the first half of a wrapped loop (Basics). Make 86 to 98 4mm bicone units, in two colors, and 43 to 49 6mm bicone units. Set aside two 4mm units and a 6mm unit for step 7.

2 Cut a 1-in. (2.5cm) piece of chain with short links on each end. Open a jump ring (Basics). Attach an end link and a polygon pendant. Close the jump ring. Attach two sets of 4mm and 6mm units to the chain's two short links in the center of the chain. On the other end, attach a 4mm unit. Attach a second 4mm unit to the loop of the first. Attach a 6mm unit to the second 4mm unit. Complete the wraps as you go.

3 Cut a ½-in. (1.3cm) piece of chain with short links on each end. Use a jump ring to attach an end link and a polygon pendant. Attach two 4mm units and a 6mm unit to a short link on the other end as in step 2.

4 Cut a 9–10-in. (23–25cm) piece of chain and a second piece 1½ in. (3.8cm) longer. Each piece should have three short links on each end. On a short link on each chain, attach two 4mm units and a 6mm unit as in step 2. Repeat, attaching bicone units to short links at equal intervals, until you've covered the desired length of chain.

5 Use a jump ring to attach a beaded chain, the pendant dangles, and the second beaded chain.

6 Check the fit and trim chain if necessary. Use a jump ring to attach a lobster claw clasp and the end link of the 9–10-in. (23–25cm) beaded chain.

7 On the end link of the other beaded chain, attach two 4mm units and one 6mm unit as in step 2.

SupplyList

necklace 19 in. (48cm)
- **2** 17mm crystal polygon pendants, in **2** colors
- **43–49** 6mm bicone crystals
- **86–98** 4mm bicone crystals, in **2** colors
- **22–26** in. (56–66cm) long-and-short chain, 7mm links
- **129–147** 1½-in. (3.8cm) head pins
- **4** 5mm jump rings
- lobster claw clasp
- chainnose pliers
- diagonal wire cutters
- roundnose pliers

earrings
- **2** 17mm crystal polygon pendants
- **4** 6mm bicone crystals, in **2** colors
- **6** 4mm bicone crystals, in **3** colors
- **1** in. (2.5cm) long-and-short chain, 7mm links
- **10** 1½-in. (3.8cm) head pins
- **2** 5mm jump rings
- pair of earring wires
- chainnose pliers
- diagonal wire cutters
- roundnose pliers

1 **earrings** • For each earring: On a head pin, string a 4mm bicone crystal. Make the first half of a wrapped loop (Basics). Make three 4mm units and two 6mm units. Complete the wraps on one 4mm unit.

Attach the loops of the two remaining 4mm units and complete the wraps. Attach a 6mm unit to the loop of a 4mm unit. Complete the wraps.

2 Cut a piece of chain with one long link and two short links. Open a jump ring (Basics). Attach a polygon pendant and the end short link. Close the jump ring.

3 Open the loop of an earring wire (Basics). Attach a 4mm unit, a loop of the connected unit, and the dangle. Close the loop.

Krystallos
ladder

Create a cool cuff of crystals and pearls

by Rachel Nelson-Smith

The word "crystal" comes from the Greek "krystallos," meaning "ice." This cuff bracelet, however, is guaranteed to generate some fashion heat. Crystals and pearls create a free-form ladder that will bring you out of the cold and into the heights of style.

1 Find a round object approximately the desired diameter of your cuff. Wrap an 18-in. (46cm) piece of 16-gauge wire around the object. Bend the wire down at a right angle with chainnose pliers, leaving a 1¼-in. (3.2cm) opening.

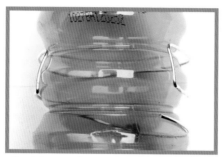

2 Make a right-angle bend about ¾ in. (1.9cm) from the first bend, and wrap the wire back around the object.
   Bend the wire up at a right angle, keeping the 1¼-in. (3.2cm) opening.
   Make a right-angle bend about ¾ in. (1.9cm) from the last bend. Leaving a ½-in. (1.3cm) overlap of the ends, trim the excess wire.

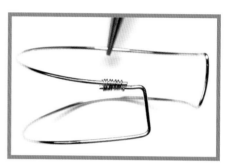

3 Cut a 3-in. (7.6cm) piece of 24-gauge wire. Tightly wrap the wire around the overlapping ends of the 16-gauge wire seven or eight times.

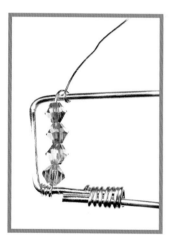

4 Tightly wrap 26-gauge wire two or three times around the bottom 16-gauge wire at one end of the cuff. String three or four crystals in one color. Wrap the 26-gauge wire around the top wire several times and then around the bottom wire.

5 Continue stringing three or four crystals in alternating colors for five columns, then string one or two pearls. Repeat this pattern to the end of the cuff.

6 Wrap the 26-gauge wire two or three times around the 16-gauge wire, and trim the excess.

SupplyList

bracelet
- **90–140** 4mm bicone crystals, in **2** colors
- **6–12** 8mm or 12mm pearls
- 18 in. (46cm) 16-gauge dead-soft wire
- 6 in. (15cm) 24-gauge half-hard wire
- 5 ft. (1.52m) 26-gauge half-hard wire
- chainnose pliers
- diagonal wire cutters
- roundnose pliers

Crystallize
a tourmaline theme

Emulate the look of gemstones with bicones

by Leah Hanoud

The color gradations in watermelon tourmaline inspired this crystal creation, which combines crystals in shades of olive, red, and pink in a simple pattern. Though the design is bold, the colors are subtle and muted. Find your own inspiration and blend beautiful colors!

1 **earrings** • On a head pin, string a 5mm, a 4mm, and a 3mm bicone crystal. Using the largest part of your roundnose pliers, make the first half of a wrapped loop (Basics).

2 Attach the bead unit and a diamond-shaped link. Complete the wraps.

3 Open the loop of an earring wire (Basics). Attach the dangle and close the loop. Make a second earring.

This necklace is easier than it looks: String the same pattern on each strand.

2

Attach cones, a clasp, and a chain extender (Finishing with cones, p. 48).

1

necklace
Cut nine pieces of beading wire (Basics). On each wire, center three garnet bicone crystals. On each end of each wire, string the following bicone crystals: seven burgundy, seven rose satin, 10 olivine AB, four garnet, eight burgundy, 10 rose satin, six to 10 olivine AB.

Finishing with cones

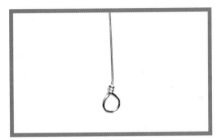

1 Cut a 4-in. (10cm) piece of 22-gauge wire and make a wrapped loop (Basics). Repeat.

2 On each side, separate the strands into three sets of three wires. For each set, over all three wires, string a crimp bead and the wrapped loop. Check the fit, and add or remove beads if necessary. For each set of wires, go back through the crimp bead and a few adjacent beads. Tighten the wires and crimp the crimp beads (Basics).

3 On each end, string a spacer, a cone, and an olivine AB bicone crystal. Make the first half of a wrapped loop.

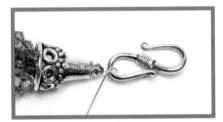

4 On one end, attach the loop and an S-hook clasp. Complete the wraps. Repeat on the other end, substituting a 2-in. (5cm) piece of chain for the clasp.

5 On a decorative head pin, string a bicone. Make the first half of a wrapped loop. Make four bicone units in different colors.

6 Attach each unit to the end links of the chain extender. Complete the wraps as you go.

DESIGN ALTERNATIVE
If you like the look of tourmaline but not its price, try a strand of ruby zoisite. You'll find similar shades of green, black, and pink at a fraction of the cost.

SupplyList

earrings
- 2 5mm bicone crystals
- 2 4mm bicone crystals
- 2 3mm bicone crystals
- 2 10–12mm diamond-shaped links
- 2 1½-in. (3.8cm) head pins
- pair of earring wires
- chainnose pliers
- diagonal wire cutters
- roundnose pliers

necklace 18 in. (46cm)
- 4mm bicone crystals
  291–363 olivine AB
  307 rose satin
  271 burgundy
  100 garnet
- 2 4mm round or saucer spacers
- flexible beading wire, .014 or .015
- 8 in. (20cm) 22-gauge half-hard wire
- 4 1½-in. (3.8cm) decorative head pins
- 2 cones
- 6 crimp beads
- S-hook clasp
- 2 in. (5cm) chain for extender, 5–6mm links
- chainnose pliers
- diagonal wire cutters
- crimping pliers (optional)
- roundnose pliers

Sophisticated
charm

Gold chain and
crystal components
are perfect for
your next soirée

by Liisa Turunen

You've gotten an invitation to a party — now what are you going to wear? This set answers the call beautifully. Channel-set crystal charms and faceted pendants will catch the glimmer of twinkling lights, and the gold components will brighten up any little black dress. Need a gift for the hostess? Whip up a second set (in less than an hour!) and you're good to go.

SupplyList

necklace 16–18 in. (41–46cm)
- **2** 18mm crystal twist pendants
- **42** 6mm crystal channel charms
- **22–24 in. (56–61cm)** chain, 5mm links
- **13** 5–6mm jump rings
- toggle clasp
- **2** pairs of pliers (chainnose, roundnose, and/or bentnose)
- diagonal wire cutters

earrings
- **18** 6mm crystal channel charms
- **3½ in. (8.9cm)** chain, 5mm links
- **4** 5–6mm jump rings
- pair of earring wires
- **2** pairs of pliers (chainnose, roundnose, and/or bentnose)
- diagonal wire cutters

1 necklace • Cut a 3½-in. (8.9cm) piece of chain. Open a jump ring (Basics) and attach three channel charms, a crystal twist pendant, three charms, and one end of the chain. Close the jump ring.

2 Cut a 2-in. (5cm) piece of chain and repeat step 1. Use jump rings to attach two sets of three charms to the chain.

3 Decide how long you want your necklace to be and cut a piece of chain to that length. Use a jump ring to attach the center link of the necklace chain, two charms, the dangles from steps 1 and 2, and two charms.

4 On each side of the dangles, use jump rings to attach three groups of three charms.

5 On one end, use a jump ring to attach the bar half of a toggle clasp. On the other end, use a jump ring to attach the loop half and two charms.

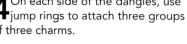

COLOR NOTES
Swarovski Crystallized Elements

channel charms:
light Colorado topaz

twist pendants:
golden shadow

1 **earrings** • Open a jump ring (Basics) and attach three channel charms. Close the jump ring. Open a second jump ring and attach six charms. Close the jump ring.

DESIGN ALTERNATIVE
For a festive alternative, dangle channel charms in a rainbow of colors from folded silver chain.

2 Cut a 1½-in. (3.8cm) piece of chain. Attach the six-charm jump ring to the end link. Attach the three-charm jump ring to the seventh link.

3 Open the loop of an earring wire (Basics) and attach the dangle. Make a second earring to match the first.

Crystal illusion

Knots create a zigzag pattern

by Teresa Kodatt

Well-placed knots create new angles for an airy illusion necklace. Twist together three strands for a twinkling tangle of color and light.

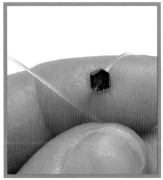

1 Cut a 5-ft. (1.5m) piece of monofilament. Center a crystal and position it on your index finger. Wrap the monofilament around your index finger and to the left of the crystal to form a loop around your finger and over the monofilament below the crystal.

2 Slide the loop off your finger and string the monofilament through the loop from front to back.

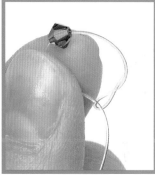

3 Making sure the loop stays behind the crystal, hold the crystal while pulling the ends of the monofilament to tighten the knot.

4 Pull the ends to tighten the knot further.

5 With the crystal angled up, knot another crystal (as in steps 1–4) ½ in. (1.3cm) from the first.

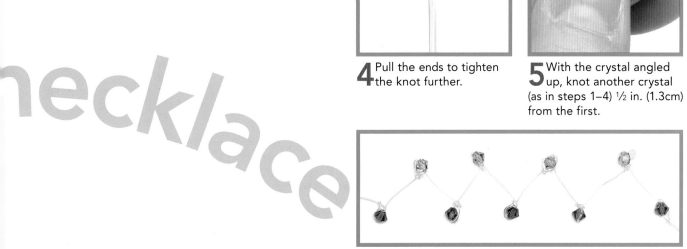

6 Continue knotting crystals for approximately 5 in. (13cm). Repeat on the other end until the crystal section is approximately 10 in. (25cm) long.

necklace

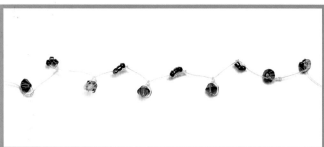

Supplies

necklace 16 in. (41cm)
- **2** 7mm large-hole beads
- **90–110** 4mm crystals
- **4g** 11º seed beads
- **5 yd.** (4.6m) monofilament, 17 lb. weight
- **6–10 in.** (15–25cm) cable chain, 4mm links
- **4** 4–5mm jump rings
- **2** crimp ends with loops, 0.8mm inside diameter
- lobster claw clasp and soldered jump ring
- chainnose pliers
- diagonal wire cutters
- roundnose pliers

7 Make two more strands, alternating crystals and groups of three 11º seed beads.

8 On each side, string the three strands through a crimp end. Flatten the crimp portion (Basics).

9 On each side, trim the excess monofilament. Slide a large-hole bead over the crimp end. Squeeze the loop slightly to accommodate the bead, if necessary.

10 Cut two 3–5-in. (7.6–13cm) pieces of chain. On each end, open a jump ring (Basics) and attach a chain and a crimp end's loop. Close the jump ring.

11 On one end, use a jump ring to attach the chain to a lobster claw clasp. Repeat on the other end, substituting a soldered jump ring for the clasp.

STACK *of* SPARKLE

Transform a piece of wire and a couple of crystals into a fabulous ring

by Karla Schafer

A crystal rondelle perched on a square pendant is a brilliant design open to creative interpretation — just make sure both beads have holes large enough to accommodate two ends of 20-gauge wire.

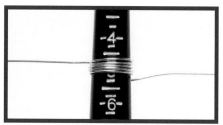

1 Cut a 3-ft. (.9 m) piece of wire. Place the wire against a ring mandrel at the desired size. Wrap it around five or six times.

2 Bring the two ends together. Over both ends, string a square pendant and a crystal rondelle.

3 Use your fingers to gently coil the pair of wires around the rondelle. Separate the wires so they point in opposite directions.

4 Wrap each wire around the band five or six times. Trim the excess wire. Use chainnose or crimping pliers to tuck each end.

5 To tighten the wraps, place the ring on the mandrel. Gently push the ring band down the mandrel.

SupplyList

ring
- 14mm square crystal pendant
- 12mm crystal rondelle
- 3 ft. (.9 m) 20-gauge Artistic Wire
- chainnose or crimping pliers
- diagonal wire cutters
- ring mandrel

DESIGN ALTERNATIVES

Consider plastic and Lucite beads for fun rings. They tend to have large holes that can accommodate 20-gauge wire. Or, for a cocktail ring, try stacking a rondelle and a square on top of a 30mm square.

Display
a cluster of
crystals

by Mary Bloomsburg

Top-drilled crystals sparkle in a necklace, bracelet, and earrings

Show off a vibrant spectrum of colors in this easy jewelry set. A few top-drilled crystals on a single wire become a quick pendant, and the clustering effect makes a striking focus in the accompanying bracelet. For a small dose of color, attach a single crystal to an earring wire. You'll have the whole set done in under an hour.

COLOR NOTES
Swarovski Crystallized Elements

orange jewelry set
Color A: hyacinth
Color B: topaz
Color C: olivine

purple jewelry set
Color A: tanzanite
Color B: violet
Color C: burgundy

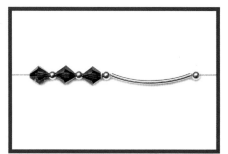

1 **necklace** • Cut a piece of beading wire (Basics). On the wire, center an alternating pattern of three 8mm color A bicone crystals and three 8mm color B bicones. Over both ends, string a 6mm color C bicone and a 4mm color B bicone.

2 On each end, string: 4mm color C bicone, 6mm color A bicone, 6mm color B bicone, 6mm color C bicone, 8mm color A bicone, 8mm color B bicone, 6mm color C bicone, 8mm color A bicone, 8mm color B bicone.

3 On each end, string an alternating pattern of three 6mm color C bicones and three 3mm spacers. String a curved tube bead and a spacer. Repeat until the strand is within 1 in. (2.5cm) of the finished length, ending with a curved tube.

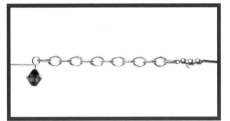

4 On one end, string a spacer, a crimp bead, a spacer, and a lobster claw clasp. Repeat on the other end, substituting a 2-in. (5cm) piece of chain for the clasp. Check the fit, and finish the necklace as in "Attaching a clasp" (Basics). Use chainnose pliers to close a crimp cover over each crimp bead.

5 On a head pin, string a 6mm color C bicone. Make the first half of a wrapped loop (Basics). Attach the loop to the end of the chain and complete the wraps.

1 bracelet • Cut a piece of beading wire (Basics). On the wire, string a 6mm color C bicone crystal, an 8mm color A bicone, and an 8mm color B bicone. Repeat five times, then string a color C bicone. Center the beads.

2 On each end, string a 4–5mm spacer and a curved tube bead. Check the fit, allowing 1 in. (2.5cm) for finishing. If you need to shorten the bracelet, remove pairs of color A and color B bicones. If you need to lengthen the bracelet, string additional 3mm spacers on the end.

3 Finish as in steps 4 and 5 of the necklace, using a 1-in. (2.5cm) piece of chain for the extender.

earrings • Open a jump ring (Basics). Attach an 8mm bicone crystal and the loop of an earring wire. Close the jump ring. Make a second earring to match the first.

Get your wires in a row

Spacer bars keep memory wire in line

by Jackie Boettcher

Most memory-wire bracelets have one long piece of wire wrapped several times, but this one uses spacer bars to hold separate pieces of memory wire in place. For a sophisticated cuff, go with a neutral or monochromatic color scheme. Simple crystal earrings extend the sparkle while maintaining the bracelet's subtlety.

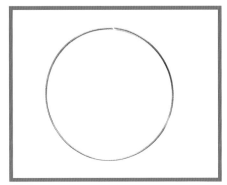

1 bracelet • Using heavy-duty wire cutters, cut a single coil of memory wire (Basics). Repeat twice.

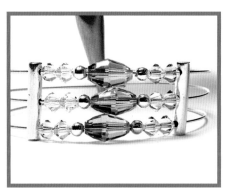

2 Center an oval crystal on each wire. On each end of each wire, string a spacer, two bicone crystals, and the corresponding hole of a spacer bar.

3 On each end, string bicones to within ⅜ in. (1cm) of the finished length. String the corresponding hole of a spacer bar and make a plain loop (Basics).

4 On a head pin, string a bicone and make a plain loop (Basics). Make a total of six bicone units.

5 Open the loop of a bicone unit (Basics) and attach it to one of the bracelet's loops. Close the loop. Repeat with the remaining bicone units.

SupplyList

bracelet
- **3** 9mm oval crystals
- **96–126** 4mm bicone crystals
- **6** 3mm round spacers
- **4** three-hole spacer bars, approximately 15mm
- memory wire, bracelet diameter
- **6** 1-in. (2.5cm) head pins
- chainnose pliers
- heavy-duty wire cutters
- roundnose pliers

earrings
- **2** 9mm oval crystals
- **2** 4mm bicone crystals
- **2** in. (5cm) 24-gauge half-hard wire
- **2** 1-in. (2.5cm) head pins
- pair of earring wires
- chainnose pliers
- diagonal wire cutters
- roundnose pliers

TIPS
- For step 3, string and finish one end of the bracelet at a time. It will be easier to keep the crystals on the wires while you work.
- When you make the loops on the memory wire, use your sturdiest pair of pliers.
- Memory wire comes in a variety of bracelet diameters, ranging from 1¾ in. (4.4cm) to 2½ in. (6.4cm). Any variability in the size of your bracelet will come from the wire, so be sure to buy the right size to fit your wrist.

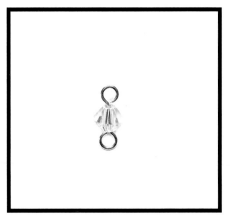

1 **earrings** • On a head pin, string an oval crystal and make a plain loop (Basics).

2 Cut a 1-in. (2.5cm) piece of wire. Make a plain loop on one end. String a bicone crystal and make a plain loop.

3 Open the loops of the bicone unit (Basics). Attach the oval-crystal unit to one end and the loop of an earring wire to the other. Close the loops. Make a second earring to match the first.

DESIGN ALTERNATIVE
For a bracelet-and-earring set that's more fun than formal, use an assortment of crystals.

Finger
firewo

Ring in some fun with this kinetic sparkler

Resolve to use up your leftover crystals, practice your wrapped loops, and just get more movement into your day when you make this quick and easy ring. Your reward for this industriousness? A ring that captures the light — as well as the oohs and ahhs — when the crystals sway with every movement of your hand.

1 String each crystal on a head pin. Make the first half of a wrapped loop above each crystal (Basics).

2 Attach a crystal unit to one of the outer loops on the ring form. Complete the wraps.

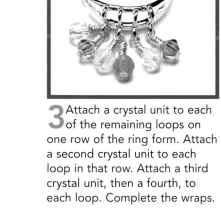

3 Attach a crystal unit to each of the remaining loops on one row of the ring form. Attach a second crystal unit to each loop in that row. Attach a third crystal unit, then a fourth, to each loop. Complete the wraps.

4 Repeat steps 2 and 3 on the second row of the ring form. If using multiple crystal colors, alternate the order in which you attach them to each loop.

by Sue Godfrey and Gail Wing

TIP
Try this design with tiny pearls for a soft, elegant glow. Or substitute other 3mm to 4mm beads for added interest.

SupplyList

ring
- **32** 4mm crystals
- eight-loop ring form
- **32** 1½-in. (3.8cm) head pins
- chainnose pliers
- diagonal wire cutters
- roundnose pliers

Groovy sparkle

Handmade "cactus" beads invite embellishment

by Jamie North

Tiny bicone crystals in crystal copper pick up the Red Sea colors of these cactus beads. Jamie tapered the sizes of the spacers to extend the beads' oblong shape. (Doing this also adds flexibility while concealing the beading wire.) Any color bicones can be strung, to make this project your own, but select your cactus beads and cosmic crystals first since they're available in fewer colors.

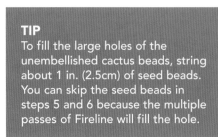

TIP
To fill the large holes of the unembellished cactus beads, string about 1 in. (2.5cm) of seed beads. You can skip the seed beads in steps 5 and 6 because the multiple passes of Fireline will fill the hole.

1 necklace • Cut a 30-in. (76cm) piece of Fireline and thread a needle. String a cactus bead, leaving a 6-in. (15cm) tail of Fireline. String 10 to 12 2.5mm bicone crystals to fill one groove of the cactus bead. Tie a surgeon's knot with the working thread and tail (Basics).

2 Go through the cactus bead and string 10 to 12 2.5mm bicones to fill an adjacent groove. Tie a surgeon's knot. Repeat to embellish the remaining grooves of the cactus bead.

3 Go through the crystals in each groove again to reinforce them. Tie a surgeon's knot. Glue the knot.

4 With each end of Fireline, go through a couple of bicones and trim the excess Fireline. Make three beaded beads.

5 Cut a piece of beading wire (Basics). Center a beaded bead. On each end, string: 7mm spacer, 5mm spacer, 4mm spacer, 6mm bicone crystal, 4mm spacer.

SupplyList

6 On each end, string: 16mm cosmic crystal, 4mm spacer, 6mm bicone, 4mm spacer, 5mm spacer, 7mm spacer, beaded bead, 7mm spacer, 5mm spacer, 4mm spacer, 6mm bicone, 4mm spacer.

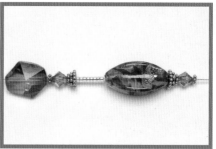

7 Repeat step 6, substituting an unembellished cactus bead for the beaded bead. String about 1 in. (2.5cm) of 13º or 15º seed beads before stringing the cactus bead (Tip, p. 64).

8 On each end, string a 12mm cosmic crystal, a 4mm spacer, a 6mm bicone, and a 4mm spacer. Repeat until the strand is within 1 in. (2.5cm) of the finished length.

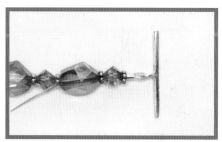

9 On each end, string a crimp bead and half of a toggle clasp. Check the fit, and add or remove beads if necessary. Go back through the last few beads strung and tighten the wire. Crimp the crimp bead (Basics) and trim the excess wire. Close a crimp cover over the crimp.

1 **earrings** • Follow steps 1 to 4 of the necklace to make a beaded bead. On a head pin, string: 4mm spacer, 5mm spacer, 7mm spacer, beaded bead, 7mm spacer, 5mm spacer, 4mm spacer. Make a plain loop (Basics).

2 Open the loop of an earring wire (Basics). Attach the dangle and close the loop. Make a second earring to match the first.

Take a
sparkly
plunge

Waves of crystals
capture the foamy
Atlantic tides

**by Jess DiMeo
and Leah Hanoud**

This dripping sand castle necklace-and-earrings set uses starfish and crystals with a sprinkling of pearls to convey the kinetic beauty of the tumbling waves on the beach and the sparkle of the sun on the sea. While the design seems to have as many elements as grains of sand on the beach, the finished necklace is well worth the time.

1 necklace • To make A units: On a decorative head pin, string a 4mm bicone crystal. Make the first half of a wrapped loop (Basics). Make 260 to 275 bicone units (4mm A). Make 10 to 15 more, substituting a 3mm bicone for the 4mm (3mm A). Make 10 to 15 more, substituting a 4mm pearl for the bicone (pearl A).

2 To make B pendants: Cut a 3-in. (7.6cm) piece of 20-gauge wire. String a 28mm starfish pendant and make a set of wraps above it, as in wrapping above a top-drilled bead (Basics). Make the first half of a wrapped loop perpendicular to the pendant. Make three more starfish units with 16mm pendants (16mm B).

3 To make C and D connectors: Cut a 2-in. (5cm) piece of 26-gauge wire. Make the first half of a wrapped loop, string a 3mm bicone, and make the first half of a wrapped loop. Make 71 3mm bicone connectors (3mm C). Make two 4mm bicone connectors (4mm C). Make nine 4mm pearl connectors (pearl C). Make three additional pearl connectors using 3-in. (7.6cm) pieces of wire for extra wrapping (pearl D).

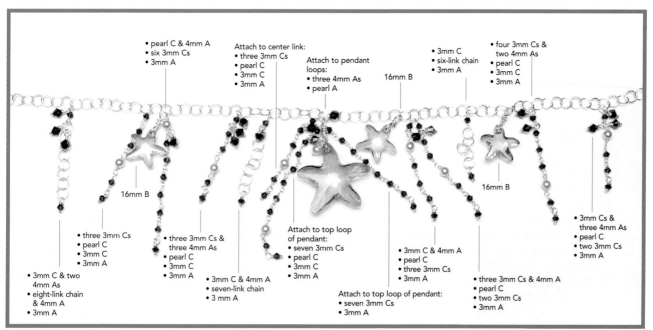

• pearl C & 4mm A
• six 3mm Cs
• 3mm A

Attach to center link:
• three 3mm Cs
• pearl C
• 3mm C
• 3mm A

Attach to pendant loops:
• three 4mm As
• pearl A

16mm B

• 3mm C
• six-link chain
• 3mm A

• four 3mm Cs & two 4mm As
• pearl C
• 3mm C
• 3mm A

16mm B

• three 3mm Cs
• pearl C
• 3mm C
• 3mm A

• three 3mm Cs & three 4mm As
• pearl C
• 3mm C
• 3mm A

Attach to top loop of pendant:
• seven 3mm Cs
• pearl C
• 3mm C
• 3mm A

• 3mm C & 4mm A
• pearl C
• three 3mm Cs
• 3mm A

• three 3mm Cs & 4mm A
• pearl C
• two 3mm Cs
• 3mm A

• 3mm Cs & three 4mm As
• pearl C
• two 3mm Cs
• 3mm A

• 3mm C & two 4mm As
• eight-link chain & 4mm A
• 3mm A

• 3mm C & 4mm A
• seven-link chain
• 3 mm A

Attach to top loop of pendant:
• seven 3mm Cs
• 3mm A

4 Cut an 18–20-in. (46–51cm) piece of chain. Attach the 28mm pendant to the center link and complete the wraps. Attach bead units, pendants, connectors, and chains as shown above, completing the wraps as you go.

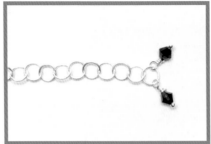

5 Attach two 4mm A or pearl A units to each link of the chain, completing the wraps as you go. On the links that already have multiple dangles, attach only one unit.

6 Cut a 3-in. (7.6cm) piece of chain. Attach two 4mm A or pearl A units to each link. Use the two 4mm C connectors to attach the end links of the short chain about 2½ in. (6.4cm) from the center starfish on the long chain. On each end, attach two 4mm A units to the wrapped loop attaching the short chain.

7 To make a hook clasp: Cut a 3-in. (7.6cm) piece of 20-gauge wire. Use roundnose pliers to make a loop at the end of the wire.

8 Wrap the wire around a pen to make a hook. Trim any excess wire.

9 Gently hammer each side of the hook and a 7mm soldered jump ring.

10 Cut a 3-in. (7.6cm) piece of 26-gauge wire. Wrap the wire three times around the hook near the coil. String a 3mm bicone and wrap the wire once or twice around the hook. Attach two more bicones, make two or three wraps, and trim the excess wire.

11 On one end, use a pearl D connector to attach the soldered jump ring and the chain. With the wire, make two wraps on one side of the pearl, coil the wire around the pearl, and make two more wraps. Repeat on the other end, substituting the hook clasp for the jump ring.

12 Use a pearl D connector to attach a six-link chain and nine remaining connectors to the jump ring as shown. Attach two 4mm A units to the top of each dangle and a pearl A to the end of the chain.

Supply List

necklace 18 in. (46cm)

- 28mm crystal starfish pendant
- **3** 16mm crystal starfish pendants
- **275–300** 4mm bicone crystals
- **30–40** 4mm round or center-drilled rice pearls
- **65–80** 3mm bicone crystals
- 15 in. (38cm) 20-gauge half-hard wire
- 5 yd. (4.6m) 26-gauge half-hard wire
- 25–27 in. (64–69cm) round-link chain, 5.3mm links
- **295–320** 1½-in. (3.8cm) decorative head pins
- 7mm soldered jump ring
- bench block or anvil
- chainnose pliers
- diagonal wire cutters
- hammer
- pen or other cylindrical object
- roundnose pliers

earrings

- **2** 16mm crystal starfish pendants
- **14** 4mm bicone crystals
- **6** 4mm round or center-drilled rice pearls
- **14** 3mm bicone crystals
- 38 in. (97cm) 26-gauge half-hard wire
- 3 in. (7.6cm) round-link chain, 5.3mm links
- **14** 2-in. (5cm) decorative head pins
- **4** 5mm jump rings
- pair of earring wires
- chainnose pliers
- diagonal wire cutters
- roundnose pliers

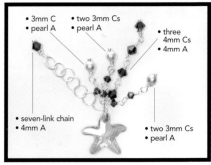

- 3mm C
- pearl A
- two 3mm Cs
- pearl A
- three 4mm Cs
- 4mm A
- seven-link chain
- 4mm A
- two 3mm Cs
- pearl A

1 earrings • Following necklace steps 1, 2, and 3, make two 4mm A units, three pearl A units, three 4mm C connectors, and five 3mm C connectors. Open a 5mm jump ring (Basics). Attach a 16mm starfish pendant and five dangles as shown. Close the jump ring.

2 Following necklace step 1, make two 4mm A units. Complete the wraps. Use a jump ring to attach the starfish dangle and the A units.

3 Following necklace step 10, wrap an earring wire with three 3mm bicones. Open the loop of the earring wire (Basics) and attach the dangle. Close the loop. Make a second earring to match the first

TIPS

- If you don't want to make your own clasp, you can still add crystal wraps to brighten a purchased hook-and-eye clasp.
- If you're skilled at wrapped loops, cut 1½-in. (3.8cm) pieces of wire for most of the bead units and connectors.
- If desired, use 22-gauge wire to attach the pendants.

Shimmering clusters

Compact clusters accent casual or nighttime wear

by Lea Nowicki

If you love chandelier earrings but think they're just a little overpowering for everyday wear, here's a smaller pair of earrings you can wear with just about any outfit, and still have plenty of movement and dazzle.

1 On each of five head pins, string one of the following bead patterns: a 4mm round, a crystal, and a 4mm round; a 4mm round and a crystal; a crystal and a 4mm round; one 4mm round; one crystal. Make a plain loop (Basics) above each bead. Make one more set.

2 To make the earring's main bead unit, cut two 3-in. (7.6cm) pieces of wire.

Make a plain loop at one end of a piece of wire. String a 6 or 8mm bead on the wire and make a wrapped loop (Basics) above the bead. Make a second bead unit.

3 Open the bottom loop of a bead unit and attach the dangles as follows: one bead, two beads, three beads, two beads, and one bead. Close the loop.

4a Open the loop of an earring wire and attach the bead unit. Close the loop.

b Repeat steps 3 and 4a to make a second earring to match the first.

Supply List

earrings
- **2** 6 or 8mm round beads
- **8** 4mm bicone crystals
- **10** 4mm round beads
- **10** 1½-in. (3.8cm) head pins
- **6** in. (15cm) 22-gauge wire
- pair of earring wires
- chainnose pliers
- diagonal wire cutters
- roundnose pliers

Clever
crystal coils

Stretch your budget with a strand of affordable glass beads

by Cathy Jakicic

Cathy calls herself "a fool for crystals," but acknowledges that using a lot of them can strain a modest budget. Augmenting the crystal sparkle with a strand of inexpensive glass beads gives you the best of both worlds. This bracelet and two pairs of earrings are as quick to make as they are economical.

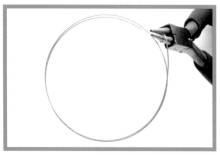

1 bracelet • Using heavy-duty wire cutters, cut a piece of memory wire about two coils long. Use roundnose pliers to make a loop on one end.

2 String a bicone crystal, a teardrop bead (wide end first), a bicone, and a teardrop (narrow end first).

TIP
Choose bright colors for your faceted glass bead strand. They better approximate the sparkle of the real thing.

3 a String a round crystal, a bicone, a teardrop (wide end first), and a round.

b Repeat steps 2 and 3a until the bracelet is the finished length. Make a loop and trim the excess wire.

4 On a head pin, string a teardrop (wide end first) and a bicone. Make a wrapped loop (Basics).

DESIGN ALTERNATIVE
Adding extra coils and sticking to crystals call for a bigger budget, but it's still a super-fast project.

5 Open one loop of the bracelet (Basics). Attach the dangle and close the loop.

Supply List

bracelet
- 12-in. (30cm) strand 10mm faceted glass teardrop beads
- **19–21** 6mm bicone crystals
- **12–14** 6mm round crystals
- memory wire, bracelet diameter
- 1½-in. (3.8cm) head pin
- chainnose pliers
- heavy-duty wire cutters
- roundnose pliers

dangle earrings
- 2 10mm faceted glass teardrop beads
- 2 6mm bicone crystals
- 2 1½-in. (3.8cm) head pins
- pair of earring wires
- chainnose pliers
- diagonal wire cutters
- roundnose pliers

hoop earrings
- 4 10mm faceted glass teardrop beads
- 2 6mm bicone crystals
- memory wire, bracelet diameter
- chainnose pliers
- heavy-duty wire cutters
- roundnose pliers
- metal file or emery board

1 **dangle earrings** • On a head pin, string a bicone crystal and a teardrop bead. Make a wrapped loop (Basics). Make a second dangle, reversing the order of the beads.

2 Open the loop of an earring wire (Basics). Attach a dangle and close the loop. Repeat with the second dangle.

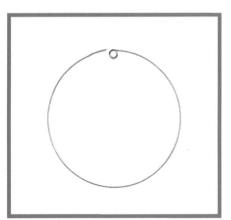

1 **hoop earrings** • Using heavy-duty wire cutters, cut a piece of memory wire just over one coil long. Use roundnose pliers to make a loop on one end.

2 On the wire, string a teardrop bead (wide end first), a bicone crystal, and a teardrop (narrow end first). File the end. Using chainnose pliers, make a right-angle bend ¼ in. (6mm) from the end. Make a second earring to match the first.

Matching bracelets
lead a double life

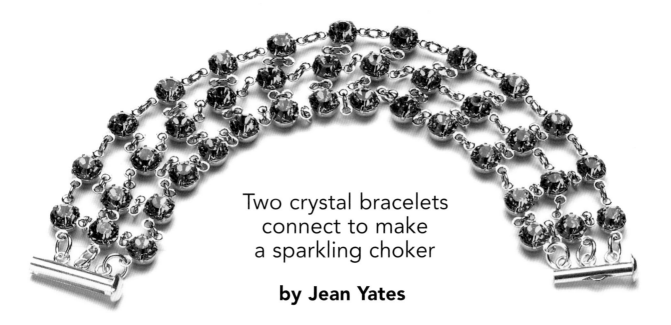

Two crystal bracelets connect to make a sparkling choker

by Jean Yates

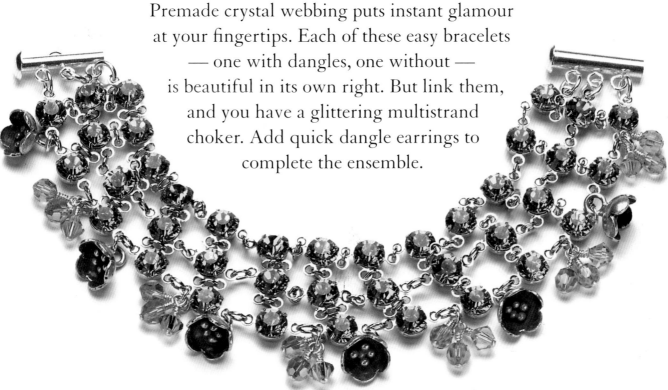

Premade crystal webbing puts instant glamour at your fingertips. Each of these easy bracelets — one with dangles, one without — is beautiful in its own right. But link them, and you have a glittering multistrand choker. Add quick dangle earrings to complete the ensemble.

1 bracelets/necklace • Decide how long you want your bracelets to be. Make sure the two bracelets are long enough to make a necklace when you connect them. For each bracelet: Cut a 6½–8-in. (16.5–20cm) piece of webbing by removing the jump rings between the columns. Open six 6mm jump rings (Basics). Attach the end loops of each piece of webbing and the corresponding loops of half of a clasp. Close the jump rings.

2 String a round crystal on a head pin. Make a wrapped loop (Basics). Repeat with a bicone crystal. Make 12 to 16 round-crystal units and six to eight bicone units.

Supply List

bracelet 7½–9 in. (19.1–23cm)
necklace 15–18 in. (38–46cm)
- **6–8** 10–15mm charms
- **12–16** 5–6mm round crystals
- **6–8** 5–6mm bicone crystals
- **14–17** in. (36–43cm) crystal webbing
- **18–24** 1½-in. (3.8cm) head pins
- **12** 6mm jump rings
- **12–16** 4mm jump rings
- **2** three-strand slide clasps
- chainnose pliers
- diagonal wire cutters
- roundnose pliers

earrings
- **2** 10–15mm charms
- **4** 5–6mm round crystals
- **2** 5–6mm bicone crystals
- **2** links of crystal webbing
- **2¼** in. (5.7cm) cable chain, 4mm links
- **6** 1½-in. (3.8cm) head pins
- **4** 4mm jump rings
- pair of earring wires
- chainnose pliers
- diagonal wire cutters
- roundnose pliers

3 On one bracelet, open a 4mm jump ring. Attach a charm to the loop to the right of the first link. Close the jump ring. Repeat along the bottom, skipping every other rhinestone.

4 Use a 4mm jump ring to attach two round-crystal units and a bicone unit to the loop to the left of the third rhinestone. Repeat along the bottom, skipping every other link.

1 earrings • From a column of three rhinestones, remove the center rhinestone unit.

2 Cut a 1-in. (2.5cm) piece of chain. Open a 4mm jump ring (Basics). Attach a charm to the chain. Close the jump ring.

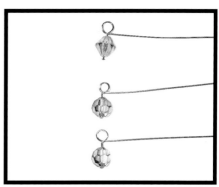

3 String a bicone crystal on a head pin. Make the first half of a wrapped loop (Basics). Repeat with two round crystals.

4 Attach the crystal units to the chain as shown. Complete the wraps. Use a jump ring to attach the chain to a loop of the rhinestone unit.

5 Open the loop of an earring wire (Basics). Attach the dangle and close the loop. Make a second earring to match the first.

by Eva Kapitany

The sparkle of cut crystal merges with the glimmer of silver spacers to create an irresistible necklace — a stunning result of the combination of only two elements. Select a rich shade of crystal, such as peridot or Montana blue, or alternate two colors for a dramatic effect. To help the crystals stay positioned in opposite directions, alternate shiny spacers with the crystals. Amazingly simple to string, this collar provides instant impact.

1 necklace • Cut a piece of beading wire (Basics). String a round spacer, a rhinestone ball, a crimp bead, a round spacer, and a jump ring. Go back through the beads just strung, tighten the wire, and crimp the crimp bead (Basics). Trim the excess wire.

2 String an alternating pattern of flat spacers and drops until the necklace is within 1 in. (2.5cm) of the desired length. End with a spacer.

3 String a round spacer, rhinestone ball, crimp bead, spacer, and a jump ring. Check the fit, and finish the necklace (Basics). Close half the S-hook clasp around one jump ring with chainnose pliers.

Dazzling

SupplyList

necklace 15½ –17½ in. (39.4–44.5cm)
- **58–70** 9 x 18mm cut crystal drops
- **59–71** 6-7mm flat spacers
- **2** 10mm rhinestone balls, crystal
- **4** 3mm round spacer beads
- **2** crimp beads
- S-hook clasp and 2 soldered jump rings
- flexible beading wire, .018 or .019
- chainnose or crimping pliers
- diagonal wire cutters

bracelet 6¾–7½ in. (17.1–19.1cm)
- **23–29** 9 x 18mm cut crystal drops
- **24–30** 6-7mm flat spacers
- **2** 6mm bicone crystals (color to match drops)
- **4** 3mm round spacer beads
- **2** crimp beads
- clasp
- flexible beading wire, .018 or .019
- chainnose or crimping pliers
- diagonal wire cutters

1 **bracelet** • Determine the finished length of your bracelet, add 5 in. (13cm), and cut a piece of beading wire to that length. String a bicone, round spacer, crimp bead, spacer, and half the clasp. Go back through the beads just strung, tighten the wire, and crimp the crimp bead. Trim the excess wire.

2 String beads as in step 2 of the necklace until the bracelet is within 1 in. of the desired length. Finish the bracelet as in step 1, checking the fit before crimping.

drops

Teardrops and bright silver spacers form a glamorous collar and bracelet

Easy wraps,
twinkling
hoops

Make a dazzling statement with wire-and-crystal-wrapped hoops

by Jenny Van

You may have seen earrings like these in stores and catalogs, but who'd guess they'd be so easy to make? You're sure to be captured by the simple elegance of these earrings.

1 Cut a 12-in. (30cm) piece of wire. Secure the end by wrapping it tightly three times around a 20mm ring.

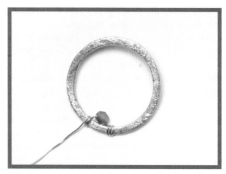

2 String a crystal. Holding the bead inside the ring, wrap the wire twice around the ring. Repeat 11 times.

3 Cut an 8-in. (20cm) piece of wire. Center the ring and wrap each end once around the ring.

4 On each end, string three crystals, curving them over the three crystals from steps 1 and 2. Wrap each end three times around the ring. Trim the excess wire and tuck the end.

5 Open a jump ring (Basics) and attach the beaded ring and the loop of an earring post. Close the jump ring. Make a second earring to match the first.

SupplyList

earrings
- **36** 3mm round crystals
- **2** 20mm hammered rings
- **40 in.** (1m) 28-gauge wire
- **2** 5mm jump rings
- pair of earring posts and ear nuts
- **2** pairs of pliers
- diagonal wire cutters

A night to shine

by Jenny Van

Assemble a variety of crystals in a brilliant necklace and earrings

For a holiday party, nothing beats the allure of crystals and gold. To dazzle from all angles, attach crystals and chain at the back of this claspless necklace (Design alternative, p. 83).

SupplyList

necklace 26–31 in. (66–79cm)
- **4** 18mm crystal rondelles
- **7** 12mm cosmic crystals
- **15** 6mm helix crystals
- **9** ft. (2.7 m) 22-gauge half-hard wire
- **33–37** in. (84–94cm) cable chain, 4mm links
- **15–17** in. (38–43cm) cable chain, 2mm links
- **1½-in.** (3.8cm) head pin
- chainnose pliers
- diagonal wire cutters
- roundnose pliers

earrings
- **2** 12mm crystal rondelles
- **12** 4mm round crystals
- **6** in. (15cm) 22-gauge half-hard wire
- **20–24** in. (51–61cm) cable chain, 2mm links
- **12** 1½-in. (3.8cm) head pins
- pair of earring wires
- chainnose pliers
- diagonal wire cutters
- roundnose pliers

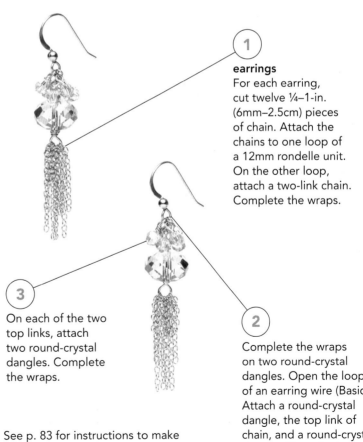

1

earrings
For each earring, cut twelve ¼–1-in. (6mm–2.5cm) pieces of chain. Attach the chains to one loop of a 12mm rondelle unit. On the other loop, attach a two-link chain. Complete the wraps.

3

On each of the two top links, attach two round-crystal dangles. Complete the wraps.

2

Complete the wraps on two round-crystal dangles. Open the loop of an earring wire (Basics). Attach a round-crystal dangle, the top link of chain, and a round-crystal dangle. Close the loop.

See p. 83 for instructions to make each component for the earrings and necklace.

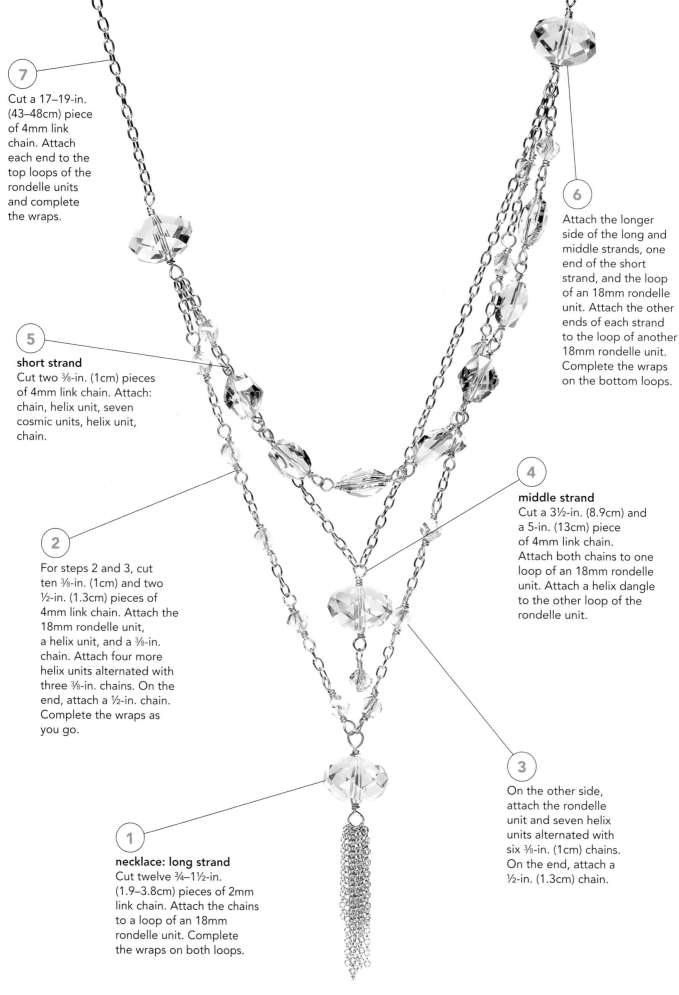

7

Cut a 17–19-in. (43–48cm) piece of 4mm link chain. Attach each end to the top loops of the rondelle units and complete the wraps.

6

Attach the longer side of the long and middle strands, one end of the short strand, and the loop of an 18mm rondelle unit. Attach the other ends of each strand to the loop of another 18mm rondelle unit. Complete the wraps on the bottom loops.

5

short strand
Cut two ⅜-in. (1cm) pieces of 4mm link chain. Attach: chain, helix unit, seven cosmic units, helix unit, chain.

4

middle strand
Cut a 3½-in. (8.9cm) and a 5-in. (13cm) piece of 4mm link chain. Attach both chains to one loop of an 18mm rondelle unit. Attach a helix dangle to the other loop of the rondelle unit.

2

For steps 2 and 3, cut ten ⅜-in. (1cm) and two ½-in. (1.3cm) pieces of 4mm link chain. Attach the 18mm rondelle unit, a helix unit, and a ⅜-in. chain. Attach four more helix units alternated with three ⅜-in. chains. On the end, attach a ½-in. chain. Complete the wraps as you go.

3

On the other side, attach the rondelle unit and seven helix units alternated with six ⅜-in. (1cm) chains. On the end, attach a ½-in. (1.3cm) chain.

1

necklace: long strand
Cut twelve ¾–1½-in. (1.9–3.8cm) pieces of 2mm link chain. Attach the chains to a loop of an 18mm rondelle unit. Complete the wraps on both loops.

Components

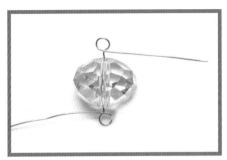

rondelle unit • Cut a 3½-in. (8.9cm) piece of wire. On one end, make the first half of a wrapped loop (Basics). String a rondelle and make the first half of a wrapped loop. Make four 18mm rondelle units for the necklace and two 12mm rondelle units for the earrings.

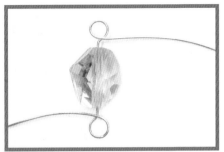

cosmic unit • Cut a 3-in. (7.6cm) piece of wire. On one end, make the first half of a wrapped loop. String a cosmic crystal and make the first half of a wrapped loop. Make seven cosmic units for the necklace.

TIP
When shopping for crystals online, look for a site that allows you to browse crystals by size or shape.

helix dangle • On a head pin, string a helix crystal and make the first half of a wrapped loop. Make one helix dangle for the necklace.

round-crystal dangle • On a head pin, string a round crystal and make the first half of a wrapped loop. Make 12 round-crystal dangles for the earrings.

DESIGN ALTERNATIVE
For a more decorative finish, make four helix units and five three-helix units. In step 7, do not cut one long piece of chain. Instead, cut eight ⅜-in. (1cm) pieces of 4mm link chain. Attach a three-helix unit, a chain, a helix unit, and a chain. Repeat four times, then attach a three-helix unit and a 4-in. (10cm) chain.

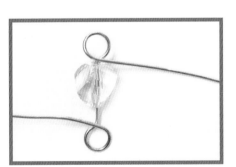

helix unit • Cut a 3-in. (7.6cm) piece of wire. On one end, make the first half of a wrapped loop. String a helix crystal and make the first half of a wrapped loop. Make 14 helix units for the necklace.

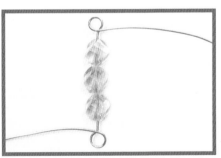

three-helix unit (optional, see Design alternative) • Cut a 3½-in. (8.9cm) piece of wire. On one end, make the first half of a wrapped loop. String three helix crystals and make the first half of a wrapped loop. Make five three-helix units for the necklace.

Bracelet colors (clockwise from top): violet mix, holiday greens, autumn amethyst mix, blues, rose and cream, and black and white.

Simply sweet

Top-drilled bicones give a rock candy bracelet a lush look

by Linda Hartung

Linda's design was inspired by rock candy swizzle sticks that she purchased for her espresso. This bracelet of 6mm and 8mm Crystallized Swarovski Elements in crystal AB duplicates the look of the candy for delicious-looking bracelets and earrings.

1 bracelet • Cut a piece of beading wire (Basics). On one end, string a crimp bead. Crimp the crimp bead (Basics) about 1 in. (2.5cm) from the end. String: 4mm bicone crystal, six top-drilled bicones, crimp bead, two top-drilled bicones, 4mm bicone.

2 Position the six top-drilled bicones snugly between the crimp beads. Flatten the second crimp bead (Basics) as close as possible to the bicone cluster. String a pattern of eight top-drilled bicones and a 4mm bicone, repeating until the strand is within ½ in. (1.3cm) of the finished length.

3 Hold the strand vertically and position the top-drilled crystals so they fit together snugly. Check the fit, and add or remove beads if necessary. Remove the last seven crystals strung, string a crimp bead, and flatten it. Restring the seven crystals and string another crimp bead. Position the crystals and crimp the crimp bead.

4 On each end, trim the wire to 1mm. Mix two-part epoxy according to the package directions. Fill a bell end-cap ¾ full of epoxy. Push the cap over an end crimp and onto the adjacent 4mm bicone. Repeat on the other end. Wipe off the excess epoxy and let dry.

5 On each end, open the loop (Basics) of the end-cap and attach half of a clasp. Close the loop.

1 earrings • On a head pin, string a 4mm bicone crystal, four to six top-drilled bicones, and a 4mm. Make the first half of a wrapped loop (Basics).

2 Mix two-part epoxy according to the package directions. Put a small amount of epoxy in the earring post cup and insert the drilled end of a top-drilled bicone. Let dry.

3 Attach the dangle to the loop of the earring post and complete the wraps. Make a second earring to match the first.

TIPS
- The flattened crimps in steps 2 and 3 are optional but strongly encouraged. Keeping the correct tension maintains the clustered look from one end of the bracelet to the other without overtightening (and breaking) the crystals.
- The teardrop clasp is sold without the crystal inset. Use two-party epoxy to adhere a #4300 (8 x 4.8mm) Crystallized Swarovski Elements component.
- Isopropyl (rubbing) alcohol on a cotton swab will remove excess epoxy before it dries.
- Make post earrings by following earring step 2 and clipping off the loop with diagonal wire cutters.

Supply List

all bracelets 7¾ in. (19.7cm)
- **6–10** 4mm bicone or Xilion crystals
- flexible beading wire, .018 or .019
- **4** crimp beads
- **2** bell end-caps
- teardrop clasp and crystal inset
- chainnose and roundnose pliers, or **2** pairs of chainnose pliers
- diagonal wire cutters
- crimping pliers (optional)
- two-part epoxy

8mm-crystal bracelet
- **40–48** 8mm top-drilled bicones

8mm- and 6mm-crystal bracelet
- **24–27** 8mm top-drilled bicones
- **32–36** 6mm top-drilled bicones

6mm-crystal bracelet
- **63–72** 6mm top-drilled bicones

earrings
- **10–14** 6 or 8mm top-drilled bicone crystals
- **4** 4mm bicone or Xilion crystals
- **2** 2-in. (5cm) head pins
- pair of earring posts with cups, plus ear nuts
- chainnose pliers
- cork or styrofoam
- diagonal wire cutters
- roundnose pliers
- two-part epoxy

COLOR NOTES
Swarovski Crystallized Elements

violet mix
violet satin (8mm)
aqua satin (6mm)
light Colorado topaz (6mm)
light Colorado topaz (4mm)

holiday greens
palace green opal (8mm)
peridot (8mm)
jonquil (8mm)
dark red coral (4mm)

autumn amethyst mix
amethyst (6mm)
khaki (6mm)
topaz (6mm)
khaki (4mm)

blues
white opal (8mm)
light sapphire (8mm)
air blue opal (8mm)
aquamarine (8mm)
Montana (4mm)

rose and cream
light rose satin (6mm)
sand opal (6mm)
light Colorado topaz (6mm)
sand opal (4mm)

black and white
jet (6mm)
black diamond (6mm)
crystal (6mm)
white opal (6mm)
jet (4mm)

Contributors

Patrica Bartlein is co-owner of Northwest Beads in Menomonee Falls, Wis. She enjoys teaching and inspiring customers of all ages to bead. Contact her at Northwest Beads at 262-255-4740, or visit northwestbeads.com.

Mary Bloomberg discovered beading as a way to create and relax at the same time. She has a home studio and teaches classes in Kennewick, Wash., and designs kits for others beaders to create their own jewelry. Visit her website, treasurechestbeads.com.

Jackie Boettcher is often inspired by her wardrobe when it comes to creating jewelry. If she has an outfit with no jewelry to match, she challenges herself to make something that goes with that outfit — and some of her other clothes, too. Contact her at jackboe1@yahoo.com.

Contact **Lauren Branca** at A Grain of Sand, 704-660-3125 or suzanne@agrainofsand.com, or visit agrainofsand.com.

Jenna Colyar-Cooper has been beading since she was a little girl, and since graduating from Western Washington University with a degree in art history, has continued to pursue her love of beads and jewelry. Contact Jenna via email at info@fusionbeads.com.

Jess DiMeo loves the creative environment at Turquoise-String Beads in Fall River, Mass., where she works and creates with her best friend, Leah Hanoud. Contact her at turq2000@turquoise-stringbeads.com.

Sue Godfrey's jewelry designs are available in several art jewelry boutiques in Wisconsin. She works and teaches at Midwest Beads in Brookfield, Wis. Contact her in care of Kalmbach Books.

Katie Hacker and her husband live in the country with their sweet children, enthusiastic dog, opinionated cat, and an assortment of farm critters. Aside from teaching workshops and hosting *Beads, Baubles, and Jewels* on public television, Katie writes; her books have sold more than a half-million copies. Visit her blog, katiehacker.blogspot.com, or her website, katiehacker.com.

Leah Hanoud has been beading for more than 15 years and has a B.F.A. with a concentration in jewelry and metalsmithing from the University of Massachusetts. She has worked her entire beading career at Turquoise-String Beads in Fall River, Mass. Contact Leah at 508-677-1877 or turq2000@turquoise-stringbeads.com, or visit turquoise-stringbeads.com.

Linda Hartung is co-owner of Alacarte Clasps™ and WireLace®, and a designer/teacher and Ambassador for CREATE YOUR STYLE with SWAROVSKI ELEMENTS. Her designs and techniques have been featured on the television show *Beads, Baubles, and Jewels*, as well as many beading and jewelry-making publications around the world. Contact her via e-mail at linda@alacarteclasps.com, or visit her websites, alacarteclasps.com or wirelace.com.

Contact **Catherine Hodge** at catherinemarissa@yahoo.com, or visit her online at catherinemarissa.etsy.com.

Cathy Jakicic is Editor of *Bead Style* magazine and the author of the book *Hip Handmade Memory Jewelry*. She has been creating jewelry for more than 15 years. Contact her via email at cjakicic@Bead Style.com.

Eva Kapitany began making jewelry when, instead of prescribing medication, her doctor suggested she find a fun activity to ease her depression. Her husband saw her beading one day and told her, "Whatever you're doing, keep doing it, 'cause I've never seen you happier." Contact Eva in care of Kalmbach Books.

Teresa Kodatt makes beads and jewelry and teaches at her store, Pumpkin Glass, in Morton, Ill. Contact her via email at teresa@pumpkinglass.com, or visit her website, pumpkinglass.com.

Irina Miech is an artist, teacher, and the author of eight books on jewelry making. She also oversees her retail bead supply business and classroom studio, Eclectica and The Bead Studio in Brookfield, Wis., where she teaches classes in beading, wirework, and metal clay. Contact Irina at Eclectica, 262-641-0910, or via e-mail at eclecticainfo@sbcglobal.net.

Rachel Nelson-Smith is a master beadweaver, teacher, author, technical editor, and digital artist at 17th Avenue Studios in Santa Cruz, Calif. Contact her via email at contact@rachelnelsonsmith.com, or visit her website, rachelnelsonsmith.com.

Jamie North is an avid beader, jewelry designer, and beading instructor in Calgary, Alberta, Canada, with several of her designs now available in kit form. Contact Jamie through her website, glitznkitz.com.

Contact **Leah Rose Nowicki** in care of Kalmbach Books.

Observing others' clothing color combinations inspires **Jennifer Ortiz**'s beading designs. Contact her at jenortiz794@yahoo.com.

Designer **Karla Schafer** works part-time with Auntie's Beads (auntiesbeads.com), and leads the Karla Kam program, free online instructional beading videos. She is currently working with her sister in their new venture, ecoFashionistas Jewelry and More. Contact Karla via email at karla@ecofashionistasjewelry.com or visit ecofashionistasjewelry.com.

A former public school instructor, **Kim St. Jean** now combines her love of teaching with her creative talent as a jewelry maker. She teaches metalworking and other jewelry-making techniques at an array of venues across the U.S. and, when she's not traveling, at her studio in Myrtle Beach, S.C. Kim is the author of *Mixed Metal Mania* and *Metal Magic*. Contact her via email at kim@kimstjean.com, or through her website, kimstjean.com.

Liisa Turunen, Head Designer and Instructor at Crystal Creations Bead Institute in West Palm Beach, Fla., has been beading for over 15 years, and says she is inspired by her mother: "My mom is very precise in her beading and helps me take some wild designs and give them structure." Contact Liisa at 561-649-9909 or via email at info@beadsgonewild.com, or visit beadsgonewild.com.

A microbiologist and jewelry designer based in Huntington Beach, Calif., **Jenny Van** is a frequent contributor to *Bead&Button* and *Bead Style* magazines. Contact her via email at jenny@beadsj.com, or visit her website, beadsj.com.

Suzanne Walters lives in Canon City, Colo. Her favorite jewelry-making materials are crystals and metal: "I like the juxaposition of the delicate with the bold," she says. Contact Suzanne via email at zannewalters@gmail.com, or visit Suzanne's Design Studio online at mimisgems.com.

Contact **Gail Wing** in care of Kalmbach Books.

Jean Yates of Westchester County, N.Y., is the author the jewelry-design book, *Links*. Her specialty is wirework integrating polymer and lampworked beads. To contact her or to see her designs, visit her blog, prettykittydogmoonjewelry.blogspot.com.

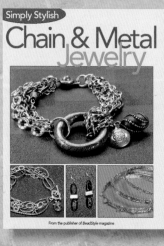